LOCAL HISTORY
REFERENCE COLLECTIONS
FOR PUBLIC LIBRARIES

ALA GUIDES FOR THE BUSY LIBRARIAN

LOCAL HISTORY REFERENCE COLLECTIONS FOR PUBLIC LIBRARIES

KATHY MARQUIS and LESLIE WAGGENER

AN IMPRINT OF THE
AMERICAN LIBRARY ASSOCIATION
CHICAGO   2015

KATHY MARQUIS is public services librarian at the Albany County Public Library in Laramie, Wyoming. In her nearly forty years as an archivist and librarian, she has directed reference in a wide variety of settings, including a large state historical society, university archives, and special collections. She loves finding ways to connect patrons with historical materials that they will enjoy or find useful—or both.

LESLIE WAGGENER is an archivist at the University of Wyoming's American Heritage Center (AHC). Over the fourteen years she has been at the AHC, she has worked with all types of historical materials in areas of reference, processing, and acquisition.

ALA Editions purchases fund advocacy, awareness, and accreditation programs for library professionals worldwide.

© 2015 by the American Library Association

Extensive effort has gone into ensuring the reliability of the information in this book; however, the publisher makes no warranty, express or implied, with respect to the material contained herein.

ISBN: 978-0-8389-1331-4 (paper)

Library of Congress Cataloging-in-Publication Data

Marquis, Kathy.
    Local history reference collections for public libraries / by Kathy Marquis and Leslie Waggener.
        pages   cm
    Includes bibliographical references and index.
    ISBN 978-0-8389-1331-4
    1. Libraries—United States—Special collections—Local history materials. 2. Local history—Bibliography—Methodology. 3. United States—History, Local—Bibliography—Methodology. 4. Historical libraries—United States. I. Waggener, Leslie. II. Title.
    Z688.L8M38 2015
    025.2′1—dc23   2015008699

Book design by Casey Bayer. Imagery © Shutterstock, Inc.

Text composition in the Charis SIL and Soho Gothic typefaces by Dianne M. Rooney.

♾ This paper meets the requirements of ANSI/NISO Z39.48–1992 (Permanence of Paper).

Printed in the United States of America

19 18 17 16 15   5 4 3 2 1

Leslie would like to thank her husband, Robert, for his love, patience, and friendship through this project, for his help with editing, and for putting up with a Type A for all these years.

Kathy would like to thank her husband, Mark, whose support and love, editorial suggestions, and belief in the importance of this project have meant so much to her.

CONTENTS

ACKNOWLEDGMENTS

OUR SINCERE THANKS to former ALA Editions editor Stephanie Zvirin for encouraging us to attempt this book and to ALA Editions editor Jamie Santoro who took over the helm and kept us on task with much grace and patience. We would also like to thank these wonderful librarians for sharing resources and for their valuable advice:

- Elaine Hayes, assistant manager/Special Collections librarian, Laramie County (Wyoming) Library System
- Nancy Jennings, History Department librarian, Johnson County (Wyoming) Public Library
- Debby Nitz, resource librarian, Northfield (Minnesota) Public Library
- Kathleen Reilly, local history and Melville Collections supervisor, Berkshire Athenaeum, Pittsfield (Massachusetts) Public Library
- Peggy Shaughnessy, web applications developer, Poudre River (Colorado) Public Library District
- Judy Slack, Wyoming Room librarian, Sheridan County (Wyoming) Fulmer Public Library
- Lesley Struc, curator, Local History Archive at the Fort Collins (Colorado) Museum of Discovery

INTRODUCTION

Why "Local History Reference Collection"?

IF ALL NEWS is local—or if what grabs your interest is the local aspect of news—then the same can be said of all history. If you move to a new house, you probably want to know who else lived there. If your church has an anniversary, it's fun to look at how small the congregation once was, lists of pastors ("Hey, that's the guy who married us!"), and pamphlets with photos of previous building locations. If your Cub Scout troop needs a history activity, what could be better than looking at the newspapers from the day each member was born?

In their influential book, *Nearby History*, David Kyvig and Myron A. Marty outline all the reasons why local or "nearby" history has become an integral part of modern historical studies.[1] They mention the "New Social History" movement of the 1960s that redirected historians to study our past "from the bottom up," rather than simply studying leaders and national events. And, they add,

> The emotional rewards of learning about a past which has plainly and directly affected one's own life cannot be duplicated by any other type of historical inquiry. It can be exciting to understand for the first time why your grandparents treated your parents in a certain way, why your community developed certain traditions, why your corporation adopted specific practices, why your civic organization became involved with particular issues. It can be satisfying to feel oneself part of something larger and more lasting than the moment, something that stretches both backward and forward in time.[2]

In addition to historians focusing on ordinary people's lives, two other developments in the 1970s gave rise to a nationwide interest in local and family history. The first was the publication of Alex Haley's book (and subsequently the television miniseries version) *Roots*. A multigenerational study of an African American family from its slave origins, *Roots* sparked a national fascination with family history that still continues. The United States Bicentennial celebrations, beginning in 1976, also led to a multitude of commemorative histories of communities and organizations. Between these two movements, a wealth of new locally published books, pamphlets, plays, biographies, and other works themselves gave rise to many "local history sections" in community libraries. It reminded librarians that they had an opportunity to document their local areas by retaining those publications even when they were no longer current.

Nearby History is essentially a manual for researching local history, whether for professional historians, or enthusiasts pursuing these questions in their spare time. The authors include several chapters devoted to the types of sources that will be useful for this study. They frequently mention public libraries as places where local history materials are collected and made available, and librarians who "often have more information about documents pertaining to the nearby area than even the finest reference works or card catalogs." Reading this book as librarians and archivists, our natural inclination was to wish for a manual for ourselves: how should such a helpful collection be assembled and managed?

This book began as a 2011 article for *Public Libraries* magazine.[3] When we were asked to propose a book-length version of our article, we were excited to have the chance to explore in-depth issues that we had merely mentioned in our article, things like collection development policies, integration of the collection into the library's main catalog, and promotion and marketing to new audiences.

As we had in our initial effort, we were eager to promote a simpler, less costly or time-consuming approach to the library local history collection. We were aware that many public libraries had basically drifted into collecting unpublished materials, often through gifts of items or collections from patrons. We knew that some libraries successfully developed what were essentially small archival repositories run by trained archivists, using the enhanced security and handling and access methods that unique materials require. But we also knew that other "special collections" became either a burden to their host libraries to handle appropriately—or were prey to the theft and misfiling that can happen to any materials on the open shelves.

We knew there was an alternative. What we have come to call the Local History Reference Collection, or LHRC, is the type of resource area that just about any library can easily assemble and maintain. The focus is on published materials: books, periodicals (including newspapers), pamphlets, and print ephemera. Many of these, though certainly not all, might be donated to the library from the people or groups that have written them and would like to make sure that local citizens can find and make use of them. In chapter 3 we discuss in more detail how to develop this collection—including the collection development policy that allows you to politely decline materials that don't really fit into your collection. Ephemeral items like clippings, brochures, and flyers can be gathered into a traditional library vertical file. And all of these items can be reflected in the library's main online catalog (including the added entries created from the vertical file headings) so that the LHRC is not a mysterious or unexplored place in your library, but is discoverable like any other item in your collection.

As we discuss in more detail in our first chapter, this simple concept and the term *Local History Collection* aren't necessarily synonymous in librarians' minds. Because of the acquisition of special or archival collections by many public libraries, *Local History Collection* has come to imply that unpublished materials are collected, or at least included. Thus, we chose to refer to our model as the Local History *Reference* Collection to differentiate it.

We have seen how useful patrons can find this simpler type of collection. For the librarian reading this who wonders if an assembly of strictly published materials can be satisfying for patrons looking into their own local or family history, we can confidently assure him or her that it is. Not only do books and pamphlets on local people and institutions answer the questions that your patrons have about their surroundings, but these types of materials are comfortable, familiar, and present no additional learning curve to use. You may choose to make this a true reference collection. That is, the material is for in-library use only. This will take some getting used to for your patrons. But you are not likely to house the collection in a closed room with special retrieval by staff, forbid self-copying, or ask patrons to wear gloves when handling the items. So, in most ways, it matches the rest of your library in tone and accessibility.

That is not to say that it is less "special"! In our chapters on marketing and on the virtual LHRC, we urge you to take advantage of the intriguing nature of older information and make sure your public relations (PR) staff and web developers showcase your wonderful collection. Just watch that high school class oohing and ahhing over the funny clothes and hairstyles and crazy prices from the newspapers way back when they were born. There is a treasure trove in published materials, many of which can also be quite visually interesting, every bit as much as in diaries, letters, photographs, and artifacts. But all of those original, unpublished materials require special handling, orientation to how to use and understand them, and costly storage.

Our point is that you can provide an invaluable resource to your patrons without taking on the additional expense, training, special housing, and staffing that an archival collection entails. It allows you to place the emphasis on ease of use, programming, and streamlined operation that makes sense in many public library environments.

What we offer you is a one-stop shop of advice and resources that can get you started. You can create an easy-to-handle local history collection that won't overwhelm you and your public library. We hope our book will encourage you to develop this type of collection and to feel proud of what you are making available to your patrons. They will thank you for making it so easy to discover more about themselves and the communities in which they live.

NOTES

1. David Kyvig and Myron A. Marty, *Nearby History: Exploring the Past Around You* (Nashville: American Association for State and Local History, 1982).
2. Ibid., 12.
3. Kathy Marquis and Leslie C. Waggener, "Historical Collections: Is Adding One Right for Your Public Library?" *Public Libraries* 50 (March 2011): 42–48.

CHAPTER 1

LOCAL HISTORY COLLECTIONS

Current Trends, Practices, and Concerns

IN 1887 A brief article in *Library Journal* noted that "allusions to the 'local alcove' are so frequent in English library reports that we fancy more than half of them would be found to have adopted the practice. All libraries in England and America should follow the example [and] collect for the library everything relating to local history."[1] The unnamed author believed that such collections were increasingly common, but this remained an anecdotal observation. Seven years later librarian Henry J. Carr reported also in *Library Journal* on "Collections of the Minor Literature of Local History."[2] But he was not content to simply speculate on the practice. Instead, he sent "inquiry circulars" to 350 libraries to determine whether they provided local historical materials for their patrons. Half the libraries responded, and he reported that nearly three-quarters of those "indicate a disposition to obtain and use these petty materials of local history."

When we began thinking about this book, we realized that, like Henry Carr, we needed to know a lot more about how local history collections were being managed by public libraries around the country. We knew, anecdotally, that many public libraries collected material on local and family history for their patrons. We also knew that the American Library Association's Reference and User Services Association (RUSA) had developed "Guidelines for Establishing

Local History Collections" (see appendix B for full text) and that RUSA's history section has a Local History Committee. What we didn't know was what was being done in actual libraries.

Kathy comes from an archival background, but worked in a public library for more than a decade. Like most county libraries in her state, hers has a "Wyoming Room" containing mainly published materials. Though her library once aimed to collect any and all history of the state, it now focuses on information about the county the library is in. Leslie is an archivist, but, in working on this book, she has grown more interested in public library local history collections. We thought we had a sound model to promote, but understood that we had to know more about a broader range of public libraries' practices.

We were very lucky, then, to find that ALA Editions was willing to take a survey we developed, fine-tune it, and send it out for us to thousands of American Library Association members who identified themselves as being public librarians. (See appendix A for the survey questions.) We eventually received 650 responses and are very grateful to each one of you who took the time to answer our questions. To our knowledge, there isn't another current survey on this topic, so we are excited to present our findings in this volume and use the information to shape our recommendations for your library.

WHAT DID THE SURVEY TELL US?

Our objective in gathering the survey data was not to present an exhaustive list of all the practices and policies we encountered. Instead, our intention was to generalize about common patterns throughout the country. We asked just fifteen questions in all, focusing on the status of the public library local history collection in all its varieties when it comes to staffing and registration, scope and cataloging of materials, users, collection policies, and marketing. We also asked a few open-ended questions about respondents' collections and what they hoped we would include in this book.

You Say Tomato . . . What Is a Local History Collection, Anyway?

The first thing we discovered as we looked at the survey responses was that our terminology was a problem. *Local history collection* to most librarians means a special collection containing both published and unpublished (i.e., archival or manuscript) materials, the survey told us. We were, instead, focused on simpler collections containing only traditional library (published) sources. To differentiate between collections that include archival materials and collections containing only print material, we added *reference* to our book's title for clarity. This possible presumption that *local history collection* implies only those with archival collections may also have skewed the responses; librarians without archival collections may have assumed we were not interested in their libraries' collections. It would certainly be interesting to do a follow-up questionnaire with clarified terminology. Nonetheless, we think you'll agree that our survey revealed a very interesting set of results. Local history is alive and well in American public libraries!

To start with, here is a very general picture of local history collections in public libraries, as shown by responses from 60 percent or more of those who took our survey:

LHCs are kept in special sections of the library. However, these areas are open to the public with or without staff available (and most do not have special staffing). Registration isn't required to use the collections.

Most collections include both local history and genealogy materials. Nearly all LHCs contain published materials (we didn't ask what percentage of the collection) as well as ephemera and microfilmed newspapers. But, significantly, more than half also include manuscript materials such as photographs, letters, diaries, and scrapbooks in their collections.

Many librarians are unclear as to whether their LHC is covered by either a separate collection policy or the library's main policy.

Though physical access may be easy, intellectual access is a mixed bag. Published materials are reflected in the library's main catalog, but unpublished materials are usually not. These materials are found only by consulting guides linked to the library's website, or more commonly by guides housed in the LHCs themselves.

It's not surprising that genealogists and historians are the main user groups—listed by nearly everyone. Roughly half are also visited by authors, teachers, other professionals (journalists, engineers, lawyers, etc.), K–12 students, and college students.

To attract patrons, LHCs are promoted by the inclusion of their (published) materials in the main library catalog. About half the responding libraries display brochures and have staff members who give talks, but very few make other forays into their communities to promote their LHCs.

So, that's the condensed version. What follows is a bit more detail, plus our interpretations of what we discovered.

To begin, we asked about the LHC and its role in the library. Our first question asked whether our respondents' libraries contained a separate local history or genealogy section (apart from materials in the open shelves). Since 90 percent of those who answered have a separate LHC section, this could indicate an overwhelming prevalence of local history sections in public libraries. On the other hand, it could also indicate that librarians with no such section felt that the survey didn't pertain to them and so didn't return it. For that reason, we are not really speculating on how common LHCs are in public libraries. Instead, we will focus on the common features of the LHCs in our survey.

What Does a Local History Collection Contain?

Answers to our questions about the collections themselves were our first clue that *local history collection* means archival material to most of our respondents. Everyone noted that their collection includes published items ("books, magazines, city directories, pamphlets, etc."), which we fully expected. And, over three quarters had microfilm of newspapers, plus vertical files with clippings and ephemera. What surprised us, and led us to understand the overlap between special and local history collections, were the responses to our questions about whether libraries held unpublished materials like letters, diaries, scrapbooks, and photographs. More than 60 percent held some of these materials.

Further comments volunteered by our survey respondents listed lots of additional categories of unpublished materials: artwork, plans for local buildings, records of local churches, businesses, individuals, and local governments (including some vital records), and a variety of artifacts such as arrowheads, buttons, fishing ties, and even street signs, telephones, and swords. Also maps—lots and lots of maps!

Our finding that many public library local history collections are essentially small archival collections led us to wonder how these collections are being managed. Are they arranged, described, housed, and accessed according to archival principles? Anecdotal observations from colleagues tell us that this all depends on the training of the person who is in charge of the collection. Why is this training required? We will answer this question more fully in the next chapter, which reviews the similarities and differences between library and archival approaches to materials. But the most significant difference is this: librarians organize materials in their care item by item. Each has its own catalog record and call number. Archivists organize materials in groups or collections, usually corresponding to the way the materials arrived and who put them together or created them, a concept called *provenance.*

The temptation for librarians to pull collections apart and reorganize them according to topic is a natural one. But it's in direct contradiction to this fundamental archival principle of provenance. If a group of materials comes in together, reflecting the work of one person or organization, it must stay together. The materials are mainly understood in context, not as separate items.

The best way to illustrate this in library terms is this: if you purchase a book on gardening tips, it might contain chapters on many different types of plants. You would be very surprised if you found that your staff had torn the book apart into chapters, cataloging each chapter according to the specific plant covered and shelving each one under a separate catalog number. The book was written as a whole about a larger topic, and it needs to stay bound and in one piece. Archival collections are just like that. Added entries for major topics covered in the collection provide the subject access. But all the parts of the collection stay together in one piece to reflect the whole of the person or organization that created it.

Clearly there are many local history collections that are actually small (and sometimes very large) archival collections in public library settings. It will be good news to those who have these collections that Faye Phillips is currently updating her classic 1995 text *Local History Collections in Libraries.*[3] Good news for those of you with any type of local history collection is that there is a new and active Society of American Archivists (SAA) member group for those who work in public library settings: the SAA Public Library Archives/ Special Collections Roundtable.[4]

What Should You Add—and Not Add—to Your Collection?

In chapter 3, Collection Development and Library Mission Statements, we stress the necessity and advantages of having a written collection policy. So, we asked our survey respondents to tell us whether they had one for their LHC. A third said that they have a collection policy specific to their LHC. This is excellent news. Here is an instance when being located in the library world, rather than the archival, is a boon to the collection. Librarians are much more likely than archivists to have a written policy for what they collect and what they attempt to cover and provide to their patrons.[5] While a quarter of the respondents said there is no collection policy that covers their LHC, almost half said that their LHC is covered in the written policy for their library as a whole. Many libraries shared with us copies or links to their policies, which allowed us to develop a template for what you should include in guidelines for your LHRC. This is crowd-sourcing at its best!

Who's Minding the Store?

We asked if the library has a staff position dedicated, even in part, to the LHC. Over a quarter of those answering the survey have a staff person hired half-time or more just to manage and provide service for their LHC. While future studies might ask follow-up questions (Are they based in the LHC? Do they have other responsibilities? Do they have assistance?), this certainly tells us that patrons are using our local history materials enough to warrant creating separate spaces with special staff. Another nearly 19 percent have staff that specialize in the collection but are given less than twenty hours a week to do this. Nearly 57 percent said that there are no special staff for their LHC and that all library staff are expected to assist local history patrons as part of regular reference service.

In addition, three quarters said that the LHC is open during regular library hours, whether or not special staff are there. This no doubt reflects the realities of staffing budgets. And it means that patrons have much greater access to these collections than the typical 9:00 a.m. to 5:00 p.m. archival collection, a point of pride for many who answered our survey. All reference staff at the library are asked to provide service for patrons pursuing genealogy or local history, and this is likely to improve the rate of referrals to the LHC since a larger number of general library staff are familiar with its contents. However, it also means that security and handling measures can't be routinely enforced. And, in fact, several survey respondents mentioned theft and damage to the unique materials in their LHCs. The inability to provide these safeguards and the need for the general public to have access to some local history materials whenever the library is open is one of the reasons we feel the Local History Reference Collection is a preferable option for many libraries.

Who Are Our Patrons and How Do They Find Our Stuff?

Any library patron could easily be an LHC user. We weren't surprised that almost 90 percent responded that genealogists visited their collections, nor that 80 percent counted historians among their users. We asked about teachers and students at the K–12 and college levels, and roughly half reported serving these groups. The same rough percentage saw authors, journalists, engineers, lawyers, and other professionals as patrons. Others noted that because they don't ask patrons to register, this means their affiliations and research topics aren't really known.

Many librarians seized the opportunity to add other categories of their own in the space for comments related to this question. The most common was, "People who want to know about the house they just bought," as well as local real estate agents.[6] Others mentioned tourists, motorists, and new residents who "want to know about the area." Educational groups included parents and students who homeschool, scout groups fulfilling badge requirements, and high school reunion committees. There were hobbyists like Civil War buffs and local professionals including private detectives, landmen (surveyors), and landscape architects. The public library LHC also serves as a reference collection for staff from local museums, historical societies, and for state park docents looking to add details and color to their historical interpretations. One person listed the following: "House hunters, Ghost hunters, Privy excavators, people interested in camping and walking and bike trails, gold seekers." Another seemed to sigh as they contributed our favorite: "Local crazies." Ultimately, it boiled down to "Anyone interested in the history of our town."

Probably the most surprising set of survey responses concerned the inclusion of LHC materials in the main online library catalog. Though more than three quarters said that they include their LHC collections in the catalog, the follow-up question about the use of special databases, finding aids, or catalogs revealed a different picture. A total of 167 librarians detailed an amazing variety of special lists and databases. We were particularly unprepared to see the number of times that the proprietary database, PastPerfect, appeared in comments. This is a system designed to document museum artifacts, and does not lend itself to integration with a typical library ILS (integrated library system). In other words, libraries are paying to catalog portions of their collections (mainly photographs and other archival materials) into a system that will remain separate from the main way their patrons have to discover LHC holdings. This was an eye-opener for us. We deduced that most library technical services staff are unfamiliar with the conventions for cataloging archival material using the MARC 21 system already in place for published materials. Archivists use these same cataloging tools but add fields specific to the different formats. Of course, this entails original cataloging, which many technical services librarians do only infrequently. Perhaps it seemed easier for LHC managers to purchase a separate system and use it themselves. This whole question warrants further study, but it's beyond the scope of what we hope to accomplish with this book.

What about Publicity and Outreach?

We were surprised at the significant minority of librarians who curtly responded to, "How do you promote your collection?" with "We don't" or "We only direct people to the information when it is requested." Only one person claimed that their materials were so well used that no promotion was necessary. Of the publicity avenues we listed, the only clear "winner" (81 percent) was the inclusion of records of their LHC materials in the main library catalog. This is encouraging news to us! It is difficult to overestimate the value of integrating local history materials with other circulating items in the public access catalog. Most of us have had the experience of fielding a request for our LHC from someone who first discovered it in the catalog. It is a great place to start in promoting access. Half the respondents also have a separate LHC page on their library's website, and the same percentage give talks on local history, presumably promoting their collections as well as highlighting the information they contain. Fewer than half use traditional print brochures and in-library signage to inform the public about the wonders of their LHC. And only 14 percent share their brochures with other community groups. In their additional comments, many mentioned that they publish newsletters as well.

We found it astonishing that less than 10 percent actively work with local schools or promote the use of their LHCs to National History Day (NHD) students. Our surprise had more to do with the fact that, in our experience, NHD students are required to find primary sources like newspapers and contemporaneous publications—a natural fit for LHCs. The students can be as dogged as any genealogist in tracking down resources within reach for their projects! On the other hand, lots of LHCs sponsor classes on doing family history that are led by staff or local genealogists. And, significantly, many listed partnerships with local organizations, particularly the local historical society ("Our library has a strong relationship with our local historical society. We promote their collection and they promote ours").

Though we failed to ask specifics about social media in our survey, our respondents made up for this by volunteering their participation in their comments. Facebook and blogs are most popular and, to a lesser extent, so are Twitter, Tumblr, and Flickr. Additionally, web pages advertise the existence of LHCs at their libraries. And, though it doesn't constitute intentional publicity, several respondents reminded us that good old word of mouth can be the best kind of PR you don't have to pay for and can't live without.

In the comments section, others let us know about their special exhibits, a number of digitization collaborations, oral history projects, publications based on their collections, and volunteer genealogy assistance programs. Several mentioned that they have an affiliation with the local Family History Center of the Church of Jesus Christ of Latter-day Saints (LDS), enhancing their ability to borrow LDS genealogical materials for their patrons.

What Else Did They Want Us to Know?

At the end of our survey, we invited librarians to tell us what was special or notable about their collection. And they told us! "We know we offer an invaluable service to our community," noted one proud librarian, "and the Local History Collection is one of our library's unique strengths." The most common contributions concerned special collections of which they were particularly proud. This is both a plus and a minus. Both via these notes and in our review of public libraries that gave us their website addresses, we discovered the anomaly of single (or a small number of) special collections in a library setting. It is a matter of pride for the library—and sometimes brings either special funding or local renown, or both. But we couldn't help feeling that they were mostly showpieces. Some appeared to be well used, but others sat on the shelf and had little relation to the rest of the library's collection. In the words of one librarian, "We have some items that have been given us that might eventually be inventoried, cataloged, and available to the public, but are in boxes at this time and not used. We also have one Special collection which is in the catalog and display cases, but we don't usually get questions from people wanting to see them."

Some expressed regret at the state of their collection, or hinted at improvements around the corner. We were struck by the honesty of one respondent, who said:

> There's a lot of stuff here that's old and interesting for the sake of its age alone, but that may not be terribl[y] worthwhile in any academic/research sense. It's almost like it was thrown together and called "local history" because no one had the guts to toss out a lot of really old stuff and call it "trash." That's somewhat extreme, I suppose, but most of it [is] really outside the realm of what a public library with our resources can expect to process and maintain and it will likely be donated elsewhere or suffer deterioration in the coming years anyway. What will eventually become our promotable local history collection will be significantly smaller, more targeted and, hopefully, digitized one day. For now, there's a lot of work left to go.

Several libraries were especially proud of their accessibility, particularly compared to local archives or historical societies. One librarian remarked:

We do not do a great job of highlighting or promoting the collection due to funding and it's currently broken up into three different areas in the building because we don't have space anymore for a single area, but I'm really proud of our open access policy. We have our state's fourth-busiest library and a heavy homeless population inside during open hours, and we've never had any issues with material damage or theft.

What Should Our Book Cover?

From the responses, we sensed that a number of librarians are overwhelmed by archival materials in their LHC, leading in part to our recommendation to instead consider a Local History Reference Collection. Many of the comments received in answer to this question are really best addressed by books and other resources about archival collections in public libraries. Those resources already exist, and we mention them in our chapters. In reading through the responses it seems clear that librarians want to treat their special collections well, but have not had the archival education or training they need to do this ("How do you maintain the collection? Most of the items are old and falling apart and we don't have funds to 'repair' them."). They clearly recognize that these old, fragile, unpublished, and unorganized materials need special care. But it's as if someone with no library background was given a room full of nonfiction books. How to organize them? Should they all be shelved by author? Does the publication date make a difference? As librarians, you know that there are good organizing principles for these items (and you know to look for the classification numbers right there in the book!). But someone with no library training would be at a loss as to where to start. We would argue that archivists have a useful approach to organizing unpublished material, and that this archival expertise is, in fact, essential to managing a local history collection with such material in it.

Most of respondents' questions about preservation, cataloging, security, and copyright have answers within basic archival principles and practice. There were a few additional themes that stood out, however. The first was that, not surprisingly, many requests ended with " . . . on a shoestring." How can I digitize my collection with no funds? How can I publicize my collection with no staff? How can I provide access to genealogical databases with no budget? How can I find more volunteers and interns?

We hope we have provided some good information on funding sources in the following chapters, but, of course, so much of funding depends on your own relationship to your specific funders.

Digitization, itself, was a major source of concern—and excitement—for many. "Is it still viable in paper form, i.e., should we digitize when we hit the lottery?" asked one librarian. We discuss options and considerations when contemplating a digitization project in our final chapter, Your Virtual Local History Reference Collection.

The other major request was for information on how other libraries are managing their local history resources. Who is out there? What are they doing? How do we find them so that we can refer others to their collections? Such a clearinghouse is beyond the scope of what we set out to accomplish. However, we can advise librarians that there are many, many more local history collections across the country than they may imagine. If you are looking to refer a patron who wants information on a family member or location, chances are very good that you can simply contact the public library in that location and their staff will be able to provide information or a referral. If their library doesn't have such a collection, the staff may know who in their area has the resources you and your patron are looking for.

At the same time, this seems like a perfect reason to plug our general refrain (which you will find quite obvious as you read the rest of this book) that material in your local history collection should be reflected in your general library catalog. In this way, you can use WorldCat to find local history resources just as you would for any other topic. We are firm believers that the fewer separate catalogs, databases, and lists we create, the more likely it is that we can make helpful referrals and that our patrons can discover the wonders of the collections we have so lovingly built.

The More Things Change . . .

A sort of coda to our survey: after we completed the survey, we discovered one other, from 1926, by a Grace M. Malcolm. Her survey was much more selective (only sent to thirty libraries in major cities). Upon comparing her results to ours, we were struck by how much things hadn't changed in nearly a century. We were fascinated to see that she asked almost identical questions to ours: was there a separate local history department, who worked there, including volunteers, what kinds of materials were included, and what cooperative efforts and publicity were used, as well as what kinds of local collaboration was there between public libraries and historical societies? Generally, the responses were also similar to the ones we received, with the exception that more libraries had separate local history departments and staffing. As we have related, many librarians who responded to our questions were anxious to know more about local history collections, generally, and also to be connected to others who had built such collections in their libraries.

Let's Go Simple

Our survey emphasized to us the need for a book that provides a simpler approach to meeting community needs for local history materials. You can provide an ample resource to your patrons with resources at hand. That is the method we propose here. We'll start out by exploring the similarities and differences between local history collections with archival materials and what we are calling the *Local History Reference Collection*. That way you can get a better idea of how the two relate (and how they don't). Then we'll get into the ways you can build your LHRC—and get the word out about it to those new and existing patrons. So let's get started!

NOTES

1. "Establishing Shelves of Local History etc., in Public Libraries," *Library Journal* 12, no. 11 (1887): 503.
2. Henry J. Carr, "Report on Local History Collections in Public Libraries," *Library Journal* 19, no. 12 (December 1, 1894): 154.
3. Faye Phillips, *Local History Collections in Libraries* (Englewood, Colo.: Libraries Unlimited, 1995).
4. Public Library Archives/Special Collections Roundtable, Society of American Archivists, www2.archivists.org/groups/public-library-archivesspecial -collections.
5. Cynthia Sauer, "Doing the Best We Can? The Use of Collection Development Policies and Cooperative Collecting Activities at Manuscript Repositories," *American Archivist* 64 (Fall–Winter 2001): 308–49.
6. Anonymous comment in Kathy Marquis and Leslie Waggener, "Local History Collections in Public Libraries," survey distributed by the American Library Association, April 25, 2014. Note that all following uncited quotes are from anonymous respondents to the same survey.

CHAPTER 2 | # ARCHIVAL COLLECTIONS vs. LOCAL HISTORY REFERENCE COLLECTIONS
What's the Difference?

Amber walks into the Potter County Public Library armed with an assignment from her high school teacher. She is to write a five-page paper about the history of the school. Questions swim in her mind: When was the high school founded? Were there other high schools in town before hers opened? Was it always in its current building? Did the football team always lead the regional conference? What did students look like fifty years ago? What did they study? How did they feel about high school, and did they all expect to graduate? She wonders where she should start. The online catalog seems like a natural place. Perusing the catalog, Amber finds her apprehension about the assignment lessening. "Awesome," she says to herself, "the library has a complete run of the school yearbooks. And there's something called a 'vertical file' about the school listed in the online catalog. I'll start with the yearbooks and then find out about the 'vertical file.'"

A ONE-STOP SHOP

Most of Amber's questions can be answered by print or near-print materials in a local history reference collection (LHRC). Let's start with the first question: when was the high school founded? Most typical local history rooms will have several sources that might answer that question. They include high school yearbooks, a town history, city directories, and a local newspaper. Many, but not all, students could find these sources on their own in a local history room. For the next two questions about the history of the high school, the same sources could have the information being sought. However, it might take a little more digging to find the answers without the librarian's assistance. The same is true of the following two questions. As is always true with local history, some other enterprising scholar might have written the history of the football team. If so, boom! There's your answer. If not, this will mean even more digging, probably into the local newspaper and yearbooks.

Do you see where we're going? Every step requires more research and potentially more intervention by trained staff. Now we've gotten to our final question. This one asks the student to find feelings, opinions, and motivations. While it's possible that some of these things may be found in the yearbooks and newspapers, it's much more likely that they would be found in the unpublished reminiscences or written-at-the-time letters and diaries that are found in archival collections.

Similarities

You might think that archival collections and local history reference collections are one and the same. Aren't they both considered *special collections?* Yes, there are similarities, particularly when it comes to the reasons for preserving such materials, but there are also marked differences between the two.

Let's start with what both types of collections have in common.

- Attract similar researchers.
- Support research/casual interest in genealogy and local history.
- Materials can be found by searching the library's catalog.
- Contain print and near-print materials.
- Contain hard-to-replace, if not unique, items.
- Some materials are in fragile condition.
- Seen as "special" or separate.
- Often have their own support groups, clubs, or Friends groups.

As you can see from the scenario at the start of the chapter, the same people are likely to use both archival and local history reference collections. Librarians call them "patrons." Archivists call them "researchers." Let's hope we're not creating any identity crises! They can be, as examples, grade school students working on a National History Day project, students at any other level working on papers, lawyers researching a tricky land case, someone doing a history of their church, a railroad buff, or a scholar writing a full-length book on local economic history. Of course, they could also be a genealogist or even someone just browsing through local history. More and more, they are all welcome—courted, even—by all types of history collections.

We have said that archival collections contain mostly unique materials. Does that mean that everything in an LHRC can be replaced? Hardly! Take for example the nineteenth-century published county history, the city directories, or the beautifully illustrated, oversize county atlas. All were originally published in quantity. But, there are very few copies left now, and your collection probably has one of the few in decent shape. In this age of digitization, it is possible that some of these items have been scanned, and are even available in an online database to which your library system subscribes. However, it is unlikely that this will be true of all the rare, if not unique, research materials in your library's local history room. Keeping in mind the condition of the originals in your care is something both public libraries and archives have in common. Good preservation techniques and careful education of patrons constitute the stewardship responsibilities that both venues have in common.

One of the reasons that patrons must sometimes be courted is that the collections we create are often set apart, in separate rooms, with special access and even restrictions. It is our job to encourage the public to feel welcome in our collections—and we will talk more about this type of marketing in a later chapter. But, the "specialness" of both local history reference collections and archives can work against us by making the public feel that they are not encouraged or allowed to use our materials. It is a common characteristic that both must struggle against at times. One way that both types of collections can mitigate this alienation is to ensure that basic bibliographic information about the resources in the collection is found in the library's main online catalog.

On the other hand, this special status also encourages local supporters to form groups dedicated to our collections. They may be genealogy or local history groups who adopt your collection. Or they may be a true Friends group that exists solely to support your operation. Either way, they are worth their weight in gold.

In short, archives and local history reference collections share many of the same users, research topics, print and near-print source materials, discovery mechanisms, and supporters. In fact, some archival institutions have small print collections of secondary materials related to their collecting areas (e.g., railroads or women's history), which could look quite similar to a typical public library local history reference collection.

Differences

So what are the significant differences between an archives and a local history reference collection?

- Whether or not most of the collection is unique material and how much is published.
- Whether materials were mainly purchased or donated.
- Size of collections and the level at which description appears in the catalog.
- The need for separate space to organize the materials before they are processed and cataloged.
- Special housing, climate, and humidity controls.
- Physical access to the collections: browsing possible or locked stacks?
- Limits on number of items available at one time, retrieval and copying by staff or patrons, necessity to register and lock up possessions.
- Intermediary step of finding aid listing for archival collection contents.

First, let's clarify what we mean by the term *archival.* As defined by the Society of American Archivists, archives are the

> materials created or received by a person, family, or organization, public or private, in the conduct of their affairs and preserved because of the enduring value contained in the information or as evidence of their functions and responsibilities of their creator, especially those materials maintained using the principles of provenance, original order, and collective control.[1]

So archives are unique materials a person, organization, company, or corporation accumulates over the course of a lifetime or career, or while conducting business. Individuals can accumulate correspondence, diaries, photographs, and memoirs, as well as career-based materials such as speeches, drafts of books, research files, and business records. Organizations, companies, and corporations can accumulate some of the same materials, but their records can also include items pertaining to marketing, communications, and legal and financial decisions. Unlike what you'll find in a local history reference collection, most archival materials will be unpublished.

While some items in LHRCs may be donated by patrons, most of the published items will need to be purchased. This is another significant difference from archival repositories, which solicit or accept donations for almost all of their collection materials. Rather than selecting materials from vendors, catalogs, or reviews, archivists acquire collections through requests to individuals or groups. Of course, some archival collections, generally from well-known individuals, may need to be purchased. But this is the exception, not the rule.

Getting a small archive started and maintaining it require resources not usually needed for a local history reference collection. Here are some examples: archival collections need room to be processed into separate boxes. Finding aids (descriptions and contents lists) need to be prepared so researchers can discover what the collections contain. Secured storage space is required to house the boxes, preferably in a climate-controlled room. And a higher level of security is needed when archival materials are being used by researchers; a separate research space is essential so a watchful eye can be kept on these unique materials. A dedicated room for research with local history reference materials is still worthwhile. After all, you probably don't want your local history materials carted all over the library. But with archival material, it's essential. Remember, archival materials are unique; replacing an item is usually impossible.

Access is a considerably more complicated process when it comes to archival material. That same high school student who walked into the local history reference collection and found the yearbooks to answer her questions will need to do the following at a minimum in an archive: the student will need to lock up belongings, present ID and register, and search a catalog that will point to the collections of interest. A researcher discovers what a collection contains through reviewing its *finding aid,* which provides a short biographical piece, a scope and content note, and a listing of series, usually organized box by box, indicating what is in the papers.

The finding aids must be searched for specific boxes of interest and call slips filled out. The archives staff will then retrieve the requested boxes from closed stacks. They may ask the student to wear gloves to handle any photographs in the collection. Making sense of the information found often depends on previous secondary source research, and any photocopies will most likely need to be made by staff. This can be a very alienating—though ultimately rewarding—process. It is one of the most significant differences, at least from the patrons' point of view, between library local history sections and archives.

Unlike for those who manage an LHRC, provenance is a big deal to archivists. In order to maintain context, archivists keep materials from one creator together and don't rearrange materials (for example, by subject.). An individual's set of materials is called a *manuscript collection;* an organization's is considered a *record group.* Another *big* difference? Size! Archival collections often consist of hundreds of boxes—measured in cubic feet. Archival storage areas can be massive—and they are closed to users. No browsing through the aisles of boxes. This places more emphasis on the archives staff as intermediaries, while libraries strive to make patrons as self-sufficient as possible.

How about using an LHRC? By contrast, the student will probably enter the room on her own and select materials from open shelves or drawers, making copies as needed. While staff may be available for consultation in the room, there is no requirement to register or interact with them. Of course, we think the staff can add a lot to a successful research visit to an LHRC—but their role as intermediary is optional, not mandatory.

We hope this brief overview of the similarities and differences between a local history reference collection and an archive will be useful as you continue through this volume. In reality there are probably lots of overlap and grey areas—LHRCs that have small sets of manuscript materials, and archives that have print and near-print reference collections. But, as you will see, we feel strongly about encouraging public librarians to develop small local history reference collections and not to feel overwhelmed by all the additional commitments required of an archival collection.

NOTE

1. Richard Pearce-Moses, *A Glossary of Archival and Records Terminology* (Chicago: Society of American Archivists, 2005), www2.archivists.org/glossary.

CHAPTER 3 | # COLLECTION DEVELOPMENT AND LIBRARY MISSION STATEMENTS

Henry, one of your favorite patrons, walks into the library and greets you warmly. Henry is a stalwart supporter of your library's local history reference collection. In fact, before failing health intervened, he was your most reliable volunteer, skillfully steering students, genealogists, and others to history resources within your collection. Today, Henry has a surprise for you. He gleefully presents a donation for your library's LHRC–his assemblage of political buttons from every local mayoral campaign since 1910. Trying not to reveal your discomfort, you stammer out words of appreciation, meanwhile pondering whether to accept the buttons. Fleeting images of buttons scattered throughout the library by forgetful patrons emerge; anticipation of blood spilt by the young adults group stabbing each other with the buttons' pins brings a slight feeling of panic. But if you don't take the buttons, how do you let Henry down without him taking it personally?

WHAT SHOULD I COLLECT?

Our survey revealed a wide variety of materials gathered by public libraries for their local history collections, everything from cemetery records to "hand-tied flies for anglers' poles" to "sometimes, whatever people give us." Determining the types of items to collect is probably the most important decision you'll make and is, in fact, the place to start. The patron base for your LHRC will help you determine types of materials and subject matter to acquire. Another factor, of course, is how much space you have in your library to house the materials. That can help you prioritize items to be placed there. But let's not forget about electronic resources that don't require physical space. We'll talk about those later in the chapter. And, of course, budget is a very important consideration. What can your library afford? You may have to build slowly, but that's okay. You may already have local history materials scattered in your library. What are patrons already looking at? Are they requesting materials you don't have? Maybe this is what got you started on the idea of an LHRC in the first place.

Besides local history items, also consider materials that provide context to your community's past, such as regional industrial histories (think mining, manufacturing, tourism, etc.), ethnic studies of your area, and national histories that have relevance to your community. For example, maybe you are located in the Great Plains, an area that became known as the "Dust Bowl" during the 1930s economic depression. Or you are in a part of the United States where Dust Bowl migrants sought employment. If so, you may want to consider histories that examine that era on a broader national scale.

Let's look at what is usually found in a local history assemblage of published materials. And what is not.

What you will most likely see in a typical local history reference collection:

- printed/published materials on a geographic area
- atlases
- county histories
- video/audio recordings
- municipal histories
- organizational histories
- census records and indexes
- histories of local industries
- church histories
- college catalogs
- biographies
- maps, such as Sanborn Fire Insurance Co.
- local writers' published works
- periodicals/journals
- city and telephone directories
- guidebooks to the community or region

- business directories
- organization directories
- cookbooks (great for local history/biography)
- church histories
- local newspapers and serials (including materials about local ethnic groups, newsletters, and underground newspapers)
- yearbooks for schools and organizations
- genealogy how-to guidelines
- publications about local institutions and locally produced family histories and individuals

You may not be able to house everything on this list. No problem. What you discover through talking with and surveying your patrons can help you prioritize. One note about locally produced family histories—you may find that some family members dispute the facts provided by a relative's familial history. If an item such as this is part of your collection development policy, then it is still worth acquiring. The veracity of all the items in your library's collection is not in your purview (as if you don't have enough to do!). Resist the temptation to "amend" the item. Interpretation is up to patrons; we just provide the resource.

OTHER CATEGORIES TO CONSIDER

Okay, clippings. It's not that we don't think you should collect them, but we do recommend caution. Don't accept large donations of random clippings or entire newspapers unless you have the labor on hand to sift through them to find the possibly few local stories you want to copy and file. This could be a volunteer task, but don't accept the materials unless you have someone to take it on as a project. All in all, clippings are wonderful additions to vertical files, but they do require work to locate, as well as time needed to duplicate the acidic newsprint onto copier paper. We recommend keeping the duplicated clippings and disposing of the originals.

Oral histories are valuable historical resources, and can be particularly successful in capturing your community's social history, but there are some considerations before taking these materials from a donor. Are there release forms signed by the interviewees making them aware that their words would become part of a research collection? What type of medium are the interviews on—cassette tape, reel-to-reel, something even older? Can your library preserve this medium, or digitize it? Are there transcripts to the interviews? Transcripts are many times what a patron will most want to review. If no transcripts, do you have the budget or in-house resources to create them? Be aware that many oral history interviews are actually so badly done that they don't have lasting value. Be ready to evaluate and reject them if necessary.

Ephemera such as bumper stickers, political buttons, broadsides, playbills, brochures, pamphlets, and flyers can speak volumes about the personalities of past citizens and leaders who shaped your community, and about the types of activities considered important to local residents. Storage and access are concerns to be addressed here (see figure 3.1). Although paper-based items are not so difficult to store—think vertical file—how to provide access to the vertical files is to be considered. We talk more about that in our chapter on reference and access. With items such as buttons, just throwing them all into a box may be a simple solution, but will not go very far with their preservation. Since theft can be a problem with small-sized ephemera, consider providing access under a watchful eye. Do you have the resources to do so?

FIGURE 3.1

Ephemera can be informative and visually appealing

Courtesy of the Albany County Public Library, Laramie, Wyoming

Taking on oral histories or ephemera may enhance your LHRC, but they are not materials to acquire without forethought and planning. If you find yourself lacking the means to properly preserve and provide access to items such as these, it would be wise to direct a donor to another institution with better resources. If there is not one, or if a sister institution also does not take such things as ephemera, this does not mean you have to take it. Burdening yourself with guilt that the material will be destroyed if you do not acquire it can lead to a collection that is unmanageable or inappropriate for your library. Gone are the days when you can accept the advice of ALA President C. A. Cutter from the late 1880s: "Every town library must collect exhaustively and preserve tenaciously every book, pamphlet, map, placard, poster, every scrap of written or printed matter relating to that town, and less exhaustively to the neighboring towns."[1] Although we may want to collect every piece of history in our niche, we know our libraries have limited resources.

ANALOG OR DIGITAL

In the first edition of *Local History Collections in Libraries* published in 1995, Faye Phillips suggested acquiring general U.S. histories, *Who's Who, Dictionary of American Biography,* dictionaries in English and foreign languages, and other reference sources such as *The Official Records of the War of the Rebellion.* This is still good advice, but today many of these resources are available electronically. In fact, your library may already have them in its general reference section or online databases. Should you consider printed forms of these titles? Faye Phillips also advised collecting in all formats and types of materials for your local history collection, and integrating those items into your catalog. Although this recommendation may be far-reaching for your library's space and budget, it is worth considering your patron base when pondering this question. Coauthor Leslie has a 79-year-old father who would rather handle a hedgehog than touch a computer keyboard. Print sources will always be a winner with him. Do you have a number of patrons using your local history reference collection with similar inclinations? Encouraging them to use a computer is certainly an option, but having print sources of your most popular history resources can be a good idea.

HOW DO I GET MATERIALS?

Your library may already have some local history resources in its collection. If you choose to do so, you can gather those materials into one section. You can also highlight LHRC-related electronic resources in a section of your library's website. But check to see if these materials are up-to-date. Printed and electronic materials are usually acquired through purchase in the case of books, serials, microforms, maps, databases, and DVDs, with funds often coming from the library's general acquisitions budget or through endowment funds. For newer titles, watch for publication information in local media. For older titles, prowl eBay and Amazon and review the catalogs of reputable used/rare book dealers, as your selection budget allows. Let your local used booksellers know of your interests. Only purchase rare titles if you can provide security to warrant the expenditure. If you are not in charge of acquisitions, your library's acquisitions department staff should receive a list of subjects and authors needed for the LHRC. A "want list" or desiderata of rare and out-of-print materials should be maintained. As we mention in the collaboration chapter, this is a good time to discover what other local archives and libraries have in their collections. Coauthor Kathy was pleased to discover that the archival repository in her town was willing to scan and make available the out-of-print published local history in constant use in her library—and in danger of disintegrating at any moment. This was a great win for collaboration, but keep in mind that she secured permission from the copyright holder before the materials were mounted on the archives' digital collection!

Although purchasing is common for acquiring local history items, donations can be equally important. Don't forget about your Friends of the Library group. They may have materials for you, or know of someone who does. Be specific when describing your needs for the collection to them, and to other patrons you feel comfortable approaching about the collection's needs. Authors of local history may consider donating copies of their works to your library. Make it a win-win by publicizing their work as a new acquisition for your library or hosting a book signing—your collection benefits and so does the author. Publishers of local newsletters may be willing to put you on their distribution lists for free. Remind them that you can store their back copies for future reference.

Consider creating a display indicating your library's local history collecting areas. It could be a stationary display (on your library wall or website) or contain online links to items in the collection. Or, it could be a low-tech tabletop exhibit to take to fairs and talks. Often showing potential donors what you are looking for reminds them that their materials can be useful to others doing similar investigations. Don't forget to take advantage of casual conversations at the reference desk. When a local church historian finds your collection useful, ask for a copy of the resulting publication—maybe it's an anniversary booklet or an entire church history. Give the historian your business card with a note, such as, "We'd love a copy for our Local History Reference Collection!"

We do not necessarily recommend an open call for donations. You may find yourself overwhelmed with "treasures" from grandma's attic. Be selective, requesting specific new publications or putting out a call for items on a particular topic (e.g., high school yearbooks or neighborhood histories).

WHAT NOT TO COLLECT

As you will recall from chapter 2, we described the differences between local history reference collections and archival collections. We're bringing that up again here. When it comes to recommending what not to collect, we will mostly refer to materials you commonly see in an archive or a museum. Housing archival or museum materials requires additional resources in terms of secure storage, monitored reading room, processing of collections, and other issues not addressed in this book.

Here is what we *do not* recommend you collect for an LHRC of mostly published materials:

- institutional records, for example the day-to-day records from an area business or a local church
- organizational records, such as committee files, correspondence, financial records, minutes and organizational charts
- personal papers, such as account books, diaries, financial records, letters, unpublished memoirs
- photographs—though these are unpublished materials that we don't encourage you to collect, we do realize that many LHRCs hold them
- scrapbooks
- artifacts (unless a use can be found for these as displays)

If you want to add these types of materials to your LHRC, you are moving in the direction of establishing an archive. This may be what your community needs, and you may have the resources to establish one. If you're considering this direction, consult reference sources for establishing an archive, such as *Starting an Archives* by Elizabeth Yakel (Society of American Archivists, 1994), the forthcoming update to *Local History Collections in Libraries* by Faye Phillips (Libraries Unlimited, 1995), and books within the SAA Archival Fundamental Series II. We also do not recommend that you collect local government records, even if they are offered. Records of this type should remain with local government entities or government archives.

YOUR NEW BEST FRIEND— THE COLLECTION DEVELOPMENT POLICY

Let's go back to the scenario of Henry and the political buttons. Henry hands the box of buttons to you. You express your appreciation and then say, "Before I take these, I better check our library's collection development policy. May I get back to you on this?" No stammering needed. You have a policy to back you up! If his proposed donation is not on it, you can tell that to Henry. He may be disappointed, but the decision not to take the buttons does not appear capricious and personal.

Your library may already have collection development policies for other genres. Maybe your library does not have these policies at all. Creating these types of policies may be on the rainy day list. We would like to encourage you to think about establishing one for your LHRC. It's not as difficult as you might think. And it will come in handy as you build your history acquisitions.

No reason to start from scratch when devising a collection development policy. Thanks to the Internet, there are a number of policies you can review, although many will include archival materials so you'll need to adjust according to the type of materials your library houses. Certainly, be sure to get permission before cutting and pasting from an existing policy, and give credit where credit is due. See appendix C for a template that can get you started on a policy. There are also resources on how to write a successful policy in the bibliography. Some basics of an effective policy are that it is:

- reflective of the objectives and plans of your library
- consistent
- flexible, so that it can be changed as new needs arise
- distinguishable from rules and procedures (Policies allow latitude but rules and procedures remain firm.)

To flesh out these basics a little: for what geographic area are you planning to collect and for what time periods? Will you collect everything about the history of your community or a representative sample, or are you trying to fill a niche, such as only genealogical materials or history of businesses in your area? What will you not collect in terms of subject and format? Who is the clientele for your local history reference collection, either existing or those you want to attract? What types of programs will be supported by your collection—research, exhibits, community outreach, publications, more? What are the present strengths and weaknesses? How will you deal with the weaknesses? Will you take materials in languages other than English (consider the ethnic population in your area)? Will the materials be circulating or non-circulating? What about duplication of materials, especially fragile items? Can they be duplicated, and if so, who will be allowed to do it? What staff members can make changes to the policy as the needs of the library change? How will library staff handle gifts, purchases, exhibits, and special programs for the LHRC?

Again, do not think you have to answer these questions in a vacuum. What are your sister libraries doing? What seems to fit best for your unique situation when it comes to staff, space, administrative buy-in, and so on? Once you have a policy in place, consider it again from time to time to see if adjustments are needed. You may want to put a tickler in your calendar to remind yourself to do so periodically, especially if you are establishing a new collection.

WEEDING YOUR LOCAL HISTORY GARDEN

One survey respondent noted: "Over the years it became a 'too neat to throw away collection.' We added too many Genealogy books that were donated to the Library but not specific to our focus on local history. We recently weeded the collection and we will be developing a collection development policy to cover it." After you complete the collection development policy, you may find items in your collection that do not fit. Political buttons, for example. You may even want to add weeding procedures into your collection development policy. Such a policy can help you decide which materials will be considered for weeding; whether you will offer items to other institutions or return them to the donors; if weeded books will be donated or put into a book sale or other activities; and how to define the review procedure for items designated to be weeded.

Weeding local history materials may be difficult to stomach at times. You may ask yourself if you really want to part with those SoundScriber discs from the 1950s with pioneer oral histories. You can't play them, but gosh, you've had them for so long. And maybe you'll get the money to digitize them . . . maybe . . . someday. Weeding could be doing everyone a favor. Perhaps another institution has the ability to preserve and provide access to the SoundScriber discs and collects in the area of pioneer histories. After all, isn't the point to make these materials accessible? A collaborative philosophy can help as you consider items to weed—or whether to accept them in the first place.

YOUR OTHER BEST FRIEND— THE MISSION STATEMENT

In addition to a collection development policy, you and your library staff can benefit from the creation of a mission statement for your LHRC. And your mission, should you choose to accept it, is to write one. The mission statement will communicate your purpose in setting up an LHRC, what groups it serves, and how you plan to serve them. It captures, in a few sentences, the essence of your library's goals and the philosophies underlying them. In her book *Libraries, Mission, & Marketing: Writing Mission Statements That Work,* Linda Wallace provides the following tips for writing a mission statement:[2]

Aim for one and no more than three short sentences. Saying more with less should be your goal.

Avoid jargon that members of the public may not understand and
buzzwords that quickly date.

Ban bullet points. Bulleted points generally read better than they
talk. If you must use them, limit them to three, which is all
most people can remember.

Use active voice. Writing in the active voice can make the difference
between a statement that is pleasing and one that is powerful.

Personalize the statement. Try using "our" rather than "the library's."

Don't feel you have to start with the words "Our mission is . . . ."
Go directly to the point.

Choose words that are meaningful to your audiences—all of them.

Be specific about what you aim to accomplish. Again, limit yourself
to three key points.

Describe the most important thing your library does as though you
were telling a friend.

Write in a tone that is appropriate for your library, parent institution, or community.

Say the statement out loud to see whether it flows off the tongue.
Try saying it the next day to see if you can remember it.

Edit ruthlessly. Fewer adjectives and adverbs generally make for
stronger sentences.

Remember, it's only words—but words are powerful.

The best mission statements are clear, memorable, and concise and avoid
jargon or stilted language. A mission statement is helpful not only as you
think about what you're collecting and why. Think of it, too, as the "elevator
speech" for your collection. When you need text about your collection for
brochures, websites, and presentations, or when someone asks you about the
collection, the mission statement comes to the rescue. It's almost impossible to
"sell" your LHRC to your library's patrons if you can't explain its value. Many
libraries display their mission statement on their letterhead, bookmobiles,
websites, and promotional items. It can serve as a public statement about
what people can expect from your library's local history reference collection.
Use it as a tool for promoting the collection and all the great work you do!
In addition to being a useful tool on its own, a mission statement can help
you as you develop a variety of planning documents, such as long-range and
marketing plans.

Here is an example of a mission statement suited for an LHRC in a public library:

> The Anytown Public Library's Local History Reference Collection connects community members with their past. Explore our collections to write a report, find your family history, or just for the fun of discovering more about the history of where you live.

Here is another one that is slightly longer, but might work better for your needs:

> The Anytown Public Library's Local History Reference Collection (LHRC) promotes the understanding and exploration of Anytown's history, culture, and architecture. Our LHRC educates community members by collecting, preserving, and providing access to published materials about Anytown, and by providing educational programming related to those materials.

What we like about these statements is that they are succinct, but they inform the reader of what you do, why you do it, and how you do it. You can elaborate on your intentions for the LHRC in the collection development policy. What is important here is that you have captured the core purpose of your collection.

We're not saying it's easy to come up with a successful mission statement. But there are many resources out there to help you create one. Mission statements are not unique to libraries, so, in addition to library-based resources, articles on writing them for businesses or nonprofit organizations can often contain useful ideas and information. Many of these articles are easily accessed online! Look at the bibliography to learn about helpful tools for writing a mission statement. Once the statement is complete, you will find yourself turning to it again and again for various needs, and even for inspiration.

READY, SET, COLLECT

We hope that we've encouraged you to acquire a range of mostly published materials that is both easy to care for and useful to your patrons. No need to stretch outside your budget and resources to create a worthwhile local history reference collection. It is worth your time and effort to put in writing both a collection development policy and mission statement. You will find yourself referring to them frequently, especially as you build your set of materials and publicize them. And as you deal with your own "Henrys" who want you to acquire items outside the scope of your library's resources.

NOTES

1. C. A. Cutter quoted in Henry J. Carr, "Report on Local History Collections in Public Libraries," *Library Journal* 19, no. 12 (December 1, 1894): 151.
2. Linda Wallace, *Libraries, Mission & Marketing: Writing Mission Statements That Work* (Chicago: American Library Association, 2004).

| # AUDIENCE
Who Will Be Your Users?

Sharon puts down her pencil and rubs her forehead, pondering the numbers in front of her. She has been keeping statistics on the users of her public library's recently created local history reference collection by having on-site patrons sign in and by tallying reference requests. "Here are sign-ins from three History Day students," she notes. "And here's a reference request from a local news reporter and another one from a beauty salon owner interested in who previously owned her building. Oh, and there are sign-ins from a couple who live in the senior center. I helped them that day and I know they're doing family history." Before starting work at the public library, Sharon interned at a Minnesota-based archive. During shifts on the archive's reference desk, she noticed the number of "scholarly folks," as she described them, who researched the archive's collection. When her library set up its LHRC, she pictured the same clientele. "Looks like I was wrong," she thinks to herself.

THE WONDERFUL THING about historical resources is the limitless number and types of people who could find them interesting. That doesn't mean that you have to be all things to all people. It just means that, in addition to the patrons who must use your collection (a student with a class assignment) or who seek you out specifically (the genealogist or scholar with a particular research question) there is also the general public, who often find your collection fascinating. Never underestimate the "neat stuff" factor! Newspapers, city directories, and local histories are as much fun to the casual reader as they are useful to someone doing pointed research. Both are your users—and, potentially, your supporters.

WHO USES YOUR LIBRARY NOW?

The most common answers to this question on our survey were genealogists, "Ordinary people interested in their community," and "People interested in the history of their homes/buildings." Two of the most important questions to answer when contemplating starting a new collection is: who needs these materials; who will use them? In our later chapter on collaboration and cooperation with other resource centers for local history, we will advise you to look around to see who else is providing this information to your current and potential patrons. Is there a local history museum? College special collections? LDS Family History Center? Historical society? We urge you not to see these places as your competition, but to imagine yourself as part of a local history ecosystem.

Who visits these places? Visit them yourself and find out! Meet with a staff member and find out the organizations' strengths, and what you could provide that they don't. Though this may be a broad generalization, chances are that these museums, archives, and genealogy collections will have more specialized materials than you will. Their collections will be larger and more in-depth and probably have more rare and unique materials than yours will.

So what does your public library have to offer? Access! You have chosen to create an easy-to-use collection of print and near-print materials that are in a familiar institution. Patrons already know your staff, have used your catalog, and know where the copy machine is. They are comfortable with your library's setting. It's easy to park and they don't have to register at the front door. They come to you for bestsellers, books to listen to on long drives, tax forms, and storytime. Now they can also find information on their community in your one-stop shopping emporium.

Not surprisingly, then, we recommend you start building an audience for your collection with the library patrons you already have. But don't limit yourself to cardholders. Think of the many other people who use your building (or your website) and never borrow a book. They come to programs in your meeting rooms or rent meeting space from you. They sit in your comfy chairs and read the local newspaper. They check their e-mail on your computers, pick up tax forms, attend storytimes, and participate in after-school teen activities. Any and all of these people might find a use for your local history reference collection.

Start With Genealogists

So, who are typical users of such collections in other libraries? The most obvious group are genealogists, people interested in researching their family history. They may already be using national databases to which you give them access for searching the census, passenger lists, magazine articles, and other sources. They may well be more familiar than you are with the sources for family history already scattered throughout your collection. Pick their brains as you develop your collection. What have they found useful? What do they wish you had? Encourage this group of patrons to contribute to the collection: materials and, especially, their time as volunteers.

Family history can be traced in so many ways besides the federal (or local) census. Maps, city directories, and histories of local institutions like schools, churches, and businesses reveal troves of data about individuals as well as institutions. Even community and church cookbooks can provide family history. If your library carries back issues of the local newspaper, then you have probably already realized that genealogists prize the obituaries and other stories these newspapers contain. High school yearbooks, local author collections, maps and photos on display—they're probably already using these sources for their research.

I Have a Class Project Due Tomorrow . . .

So, who else among your patron base is a logical constituency for your collection? Students! From statewide mandates for the study of local history in primary and secondary schools to college papers, you know that school projects bring these patrons to your reference desks every day. Does your community participate in National History Day? If so, then you already know that this group is eager to use your local history materials.

Typical reference questions might include: Who was our town named for? What were the newspaper headlines on my birthday or 100 years ago? Was my church always in this neighborhood? How can I figure out where the first African Americans lived in town? My teacher says we have to pick a local building and find its history. I'm studying the impact of the paper mill on our county's economy. My school is having its hundredth anniversary . . . Wouldn't it be nice to have all the sources for these projects in one place? Your collection can be that place!

Students will find you, whether you organize a local history reference collection or not. But with a consolidated location, you can reach out to local teachers and encourage them to tour your collection. Who knows, they might even start building assignments based on what you can offer their students. OK, that might be a pipe dream, but at least it's easier to orient and assist them.

In fact, teachers are a main audience group. Primary grade teachers are looking for resources when teaching community and state histories, usually more at the third- and fourth-grade levels. Depending on their curricula, secondary grade teachers will look for local and state materials to provide more meaning and impact to their history, government, and social studies lessons in the classroom. The Common Core State Standards, adopted by a number of states, are specifying that social studies lessons incorporate primary sources—like the newspapers, high school yearbooks, and city directories in your collection. A handout specifically for teachers, or the offer to be part of a school in-service session, can show your local schools how their public library has more than bestsellers and DVDs for their students' homework needs. Ask a teacher you know about potentially effective ways to attract his or her colleagues to your collection. Maybe that teacher is seeking your local history resources or will know someone who is looking for them. You're the best salesperson on what your collection can offer!

BUILDING A SURVEY YOU CAN LOVE

As you determine which of your patrons—or potential patrons—might be most receptive to an LHRC, a user survey can be a useful tool. One author has noted that "user surveys tend to 'slide off the plate' as information professionals go about their busy schedules."[1] They sound expensive, complicated, and labor-intensive, but they needn't be. There are many books on the topic of conducting library surveys (some are in our bibliography). For a quick introduction to the do's, don'ts, and how-to's of user surveys, we particularly liked "The Library Survey: Friend or Foe? Lessons Learned Designing and Implementing User Surveys" by Brown, Yff, and Rogers.[2] The authors succinctly cover the basics of surveys: determining the purpose and audience, question construction, survey delivery platform and distribution plan, testing, incentives for participants, response tabulation, and analysis. Other considerations include "segmenting" your survey audience—tailoring different versions for different patrons (students vs. genealogists, for example) and whether you want to conduct focus groups or other in-person inquiries. One option is to start with a focus group to help you refine your survey questions and make sure they are understandable. Remember that any group interaction like this is also a marketing opportunity for your collection. Simply asking if they would value your collection can be their first awareness that you have one!

The "Library Survey" article also contains an excellent list of readings on survey design—and online examples from which to borrow. As another set of authors, who conducted their library survey "on a shoestring," note: "How do you design a library-user survey from scratch? If you're smart, you don't."[3] Brown, Yff, and Rogers remind us that when we ask patrons what they want and don't want, we should anticipate making "actionable improvements" as a result. After all, a survey doesn't tell patrons what to think, it asks them. If you don't want to know what they think, you probably shouldn't be asking them questions. Be prepared to consider adding or deleting aspects of your collection based on this input.

HIDDEN IN PLAIN SIGHT: POTENTIAL USERS ARE EVERYWHERE

If you look around the library on a busy day, you will probably encounter many other people who could make good use of your local history reference collection:

- a newspaper reporter writing a story on the new high school bond issue;
- an engineer assigned to do an environmental impact statement for a crumbling bridge replacement project;
- a lawyer trying to determine which groups rented a disputed civic center;
- an artist fascinated by an uncovered mural;
- someone looking to re-create his family's cattle brand;
- a businesswoman who wants to name her store after a town founder;
- a first-time homeowner wondering who else lived in his home;
- a politician wondering for how many years the city mayor has been chosen from the town council;
- a couple celebrating their 50th anniversary and wanting details from life 50 years ago to enliven their celebration;
- a member of the local historical group writing about your town's centennial; or
- a worker researching her status as a possible "downwinder." (A librarian noted on our survey, "If you lived downwind of the atomic bomb testing in Nevada, then you were exposed and might have developed cancer later in life. With our local phone books and city directories,

we have assisted people to prove they were here during the test period.")

GET THE IDEA?

Of course, some of the patrons we have listed above may not have discovered you yet. They should be first on your list for outreach efforts. But, while you're in brainstorming mode, consider anyone and everyone who might reasonably find your materials useful to their work. Check out our chapter on marketing—it has tips on reaching out to potential audiences. Brochures and leaflets in the main areas of the library can entice patrons to explore your collection. Don't hesitate to make several versions of the same brochure, directed to students, genealogists, and any other group that may use other parts of the building, but not visit the local history reference collection. Repurposing can be a virtue. Also, don't be shy about suggesting ways to use the collection, including likely subjects for student papers. You know the strengths of your collection better than they do, so feel free to guide them toward topics that they will have success pursuing in your library. These topic and source lists are appropriate not only for printed brochures, but also for your website. Which brings us to . . .

USERS IN PAJAMAS:
EXPANDING 24/7 USE THROUGH THE WEB

In our chapter Your Virtual Local History Reference Collection we talk more about what you might include on your website. But for the moment, let's consider who might find this type of offering attractive, and who your online audience might be. As with most of these audience categories, this one includes the intentional: they came to your website looking to see what you offered, and the unintentional: a search engine dropped them into a page deep into your website and they don't even realize which library you are.

Intentional visitors are, generally, little different from your on-site audience in terms of what they're seeking and why. They have all the same types of research interests, and their products (paper, article, report, presentation, general interest) are the same. What is different is that they are more comfortable beginning their search online. They expect the local history portion of your website to be user-friendly, lead them quickly to specific information, and give them a useful overview of what can be accessed online and what will require a phone call to you or a library visit. They will consume whatever groups of data (obituary indices, newspaper listings, photo databases, etc.) you present clearly to them. And, they will ask for more . . . The law of rising expectations is in operation here, so be clear about what you can provide and what you can't.

Unintentional visitors to your website often have no idea that they are "your" visitors. If you index it, they will come, so to speak. Again, you should be ready for increased requests. In other words, if you load an obituary index, feeling pleased that you could offer this helpful resource to your genealogists, their likely response will be: "Are the obituaries online, too?" If you're looking for a simple way to determine what to digitize next, this could be it!

Of course, many of these users will be far beyond your local area. You will need to determine how much service you can give to those beyond your service area. Perhaps non-local inquiries can be handled by volunteers? Whatever you decide, be clear about your policy on your website. We will talk in our chapter on the virtual local history reference collection about how to capture data on who is visiting your site. This is a different way of looking at your audience and one you will have to learn to evaluate.

YOUR NOT-SO-BEST-KEPT SECRET

Ultimately, anyone could find your local history reference collection useful. The trick is reaching out first to those who already use these types of materials or are interested in topics that your collection can help them explore. The next step is to select several new types of patrons and try marketing your collection to them. Regardless of who else you pick, we advise that you include journalists in one of these two groups, as they can help you spread the word as you build your patron base. Make sure that your local history reference collection is not a "well-hidden secret," and you will be continually and pleasantly surprised by who finds it and makes creative new uses of all you have collected and made available!

NOTES

1. George R. Plosker, "Conducting User Surveys: An Ongoing Information Imperative," *Online* 26, no. 5 (September/October 2002), www.infotoday.com/online/sep02/Plosker.htm.
2. Charles Brown, Belinda Yff, and Kandace Rogers, "The Library Survey: Friend or Foe? Lessons Learned Designing and Implementing User Surveys," *Kentucky Libraries* 75, no. 1 (Winter 2011): 22–25, http://sc.akronlibrary.org/wp-content/ blogs.dir/19/files/2011/07/User-surveys-friend-or-foe.pdf.
3. Susanna Eng and Susan Gardner, "Conducting Surveys on a Shoestring Budget: USC Staffers Garner Invaluable Library-User Information for Less Than $200," *American Libraries* (February 2005): 38–39.

| CHAPTER 5 | # COLLABORATION WITH OTHER LOCAL HISTORY ORGANIZATIONS |

Karen is in a quandary. Her local history materials are the best resources imaginable, in her humble opinion, but she wants to find a creative way to get the word out. Not that she hasn't made progress. Since she started at Glenmont Public Library three years ago, Karen has been cooperating with the local historical society and other public libraries in her area by sharing brochure space and website links. And she is sure to refer patrons to the other institutions when needed, and she knows they do the same. In fact, a patron researching family history came in just yesterday to see her, referred by another public library in town. Karen has even done some coordinated activities with sister institutions. She smiles as she recalls the excitement of the community's genealogical group when her library hosted a workshop on discovering and using online research databases. Karen brought together staff from the various town libraries and from the historical society. She even learned a lot from that event. And wasn't it a hit! She thought the library would have to stay open until midnight.

But she really wants to reach a wider audience, and she feels sure other institutions in the community would like to do the same. What about the school kids working on local history projects? And the local community college; she saw a course on historic preservation in their recent catalog. She has some great local resources on that, and so does the historical society.

It dawns on Karen that what she envisions is collaboration, one that involves more commitment than other efforts her library and the other local institutions have attempted before. Whoa, she wonders, are we ready for this? Karen remembers a collaborative effort in which she and the other members believed collaboration was such a good thing that they kept at a trivial project and didn't ask critical questions. She cringes to think of how she plugged away and went to countless meetings that ended up being a waste of time.

Nevertheless, she also knows that a collaboration done well can help all involved come up with innovations that each of them may not think of alone. They could pool existing resources and come up with something better. They could use collaboration to make operations become more efficient by cutting costs or by enhancing the quality of their decisions. What about how it could help provide more efficient and effective services and better outcomes? Okay, that's the ticket. Yes, it's time to dig in for some real collaboration. Karen now wants to learn more about what a successful collaborative effort should look like.

AM I COOPERATING, COORDINATING, OR COLLABORATING?

There can be misconceptions about what collaboration really means. It is more than just the staff and volunteers of your library referring patrons or historical material donors to another more appropriate organization. That is more in line with cooperation. Not to say cooperation isn't extremely important! Cooperation is essential in making sure historical materials are housed at the most appropriate institutions in terms of collecting niche and preservation abilities. For instance, coauthor Kathy did a "Big Basement Cleanout" at her library and discovered two sets of manuscript materials from her state's library association as well as original cassette tapes and transcripts from a local oral history collection. Knowing that these materials do not fit her library's collecting policy or preservation capabilities, she took them to the University of Wyoming's American Heritage Center (AHC) where coauthor Leslie works. The AHC is a large archive that houses these types of materials and collects in state history. It was a win-win for both institutions. A similar scenario showed up in our survey: "We are a very small library in a very small town. Our local historical society is very strong and they house a large local history collection, so we leave that in their hands." A cooperative, not competitive, relationship between your region's history-based institutions benefits everyone.

In his 2004 paper "Library Collaboration: What Makes It Work?" University of Waterloo (Canada) librarian Murray Shepherd points out the differences between cooperation, coordination, and collaboration.[1] Why does it matter? Because it's good to know how they contrast; each involves a different level of commitment. And most likely, you only have so many resources to spread around.

According to Shepherd, the differences between cooperation, coordination, and collaboration revolve around complexity. Cooperation is the easiest. Karen sharing her library's brochure space with other institutions is an excellent example. Although helpful to all involved, there is no large commitment. Coordination goes a bit deeper. Compatibility of goals is considered and there is a focus on a *particular* project of predetermined length that requires planning. Each organization has an assigned role but can act independently. A one-off public workshop created by several institutions coming together is an example. Collaboration is the most involved and can be one of the most rewarding. Groups that work collaboratively can obtain greater resources, recognition, and reward when facing competition for limited resources. All three—cooperation, coordination, and collaboration—can be done to benefit your local history reference collection. The choice depends on your objectives and your resources. Let's talk more about collaboration since it is the most multifaceted of the three.

COLLABORATION 101

Murray Shepherd's points about collaboration are so, well, to the point, we feel we must return to them again quickly. Shepherd notes that collaborative undertakings should have:

- benefit for all the participants;
- well-defined relationships;
- common, new goals;
- commitments from each organization's leaders;
- several projects with long-term effort and results;
- comprehensive planning, including:
  - development of joint strategies and measures of success, that is, benefits to the user;
  - mutual risk;
  - shared resources or jointly contracted; and
  - distributed benefits—more is accomplished jointly than could be individually.

He continues by defining a collaborative relationship, which includes:

- a commitment to a mission;
- a jointly developed organizational structure, with

> clearly defined and interrelated roles and responsibilities;
> shared responsibility and control;
> balanced ownership;
> distributed leadership;
> mutual authority and accountability for success;
> sharing of resources and rewards; and
> means of formal communication, at several levels.

THEORY INTO ACTION

Let's go back to Karen's situation to put theory into action. She first thinks about potential collaborators when it comes to outreach to the area's schools. Archives, other libraries, historic sites, museums, genealogical organizations, teachers, and teacher groups are all prospective collaborators for anyone thinking about this type of partnership. Karen does some Internet searching and phone calling to see if there is already a regional collaboration that she might be able to join. No reason to start something if it already exists. She also calls the local historical society to see if someone there is aware of any collaboration. She finds that, indeed, no collaborative effort already exists on pooling resources for outreach to local schools.

She decides it's best to take it slowly, so for now, she'll only think of including a few partners—her library, the local historical society, a Glenmont Middle School social studies teacher involved in the state's History Day competition, and a Glenmont High School history teacher who has shown interest in her library's LHRC materials. She considers the culture at each institution, including her own. Will her library administration support her on this? How about administrators at the other institutions? She thinks they will but knows a mutual meeting will help determine the level of support from each. If all goes well, she and her collaborators will put together a proposal that provides an idea of who, when, what, where, how much (staff and other resources), and why before they move forward.

WHERE SHOULD I BEGIN?

Okay, don't close the book. Collaboration is not as scary as it sounds. Think of it as two or more people or organizations distributing responsibilities to realize shared goals. And, before you dive too deep into thinking of potential collaborations, check the landscape first. Are there collaborative efforts or programs locally or in your state or region that lend themselves to your LHRC? Maybe you can join something that already has success built into it.

Before you begin, it's also sensible to be aware of your library's culture when it comes to collaboration. University of California, Berkeley management professor Morten T. Hansen has researched collaboration, more in the corporate world, but his findings can translate to the library world as well. He writes in his book *Collaboration: How Leaders Avoid the Traps, Create Unity and Reap Big Results* about certain barriers that can prevent us from collaborating.[2] He lists these barriers as:

- the "not-invented-here" barrier—we don't reach out to others;
- the "hoarding" barrier—we keep things to ourselves;
- the "search" barrier—we can't find what we need anywhere; and
- the "transfer" barrier—we only work with people we know well.

Do you recognize any of these barriers at your library? Before you suggest a collaborative effort, make sure your library's administrators are fully on board with collaboration in the first place. It could be in how you pitch your idea. Cover your bases by putting together a thorough proposal that outlines who, when, what, where, why, and how much (staff and other resources).

Remember that the whole objective of collaboration is not merely to tear down silos and get people to work together. The goal is better results. This means you should only collaborate when it is the best way to improve performance. For some goals, it may be best to work independently. You have permission to say no to collaboration when it is not suitable for your library. And, in fact, bad collaboration is worse than no collaboration at all. Because many people believe collaboration is a good thing, they keep at an unworkable project and don't ask critical questions. They plug away and go to meetings where they shouldn't be spending time. However, by collaborating with new and different people, you may be able to come up with better innovations than any one of you could have generated alone. You might pool your existing resources and come up with something better. Collaboration can also be used to make operations more efficient by cutting costs or by enhancing the quality of the decisions that get made. Less duplication and overlap of services can result, in addition to more efficient and effective services and better outcomes.

COLLABORATION: AN INFINITE VARIETY

Collaboration can take many forms, from informal information-sharing arrangements to more formal joint-administrative and joint-programming activities. For example, the Laramie County Library System in Cheyenne,

Wyoming, has melded the resources of the library's Special Collections and the local genealogical society's volunteers.[3] This collaboration combines space, staff, materials, and patrons into one useful venue within the Laramie County Library. In Karen's case, the collaborators could work on hosting or being part of school literacy events, back-to-school events, public library reading programs, author visits to schools or public libraries, and teacher appreciation events, all as means of outreach. In other types of collaboration, organizations might consider combining their efforts to share in the costs associated with fund-raising events. Teaming up to prepare collecting policies, establish joint speakers bureaus, or even supply ordering in bulk are all examples of collaboration. Digitization of LHRC materials is one area where collaborations can work to everyone's advantage.

If you are not already a member, consider joining the SAA Public Library Archives/Special Collections (PLASC) Roundtable. You don't have to be a member of the SAA to participate in the PLASC Roundtable. You can join its electronic discussion list and engage in discussions of and work on issues of interest to its membership. The mission of this group is to "encourage advocacy for and education about archival, manuscript, local history, genealogy, and other historic and special collections within public libraries of all sizes; provide an arena for discussion and dissemination of best practices of the archives, library, museum, and history fields; and work to support the informational, historical, and cultural interests that converge in public library archives and special collections."[4] In an earlier chapter we mentioned that the American Library Association has a similar group: the Local History Committee, which is part of RUSA (Reference and User Services Association, a division of ALA). To see what projects they are currently working on, including sessions for ALA and Public Librarian Association (PLA) annual meetings, check their web page.[5]

DIGITIZATION COLLABORATION MODELS

These collaborations are digitization-specific, but the means of achieving their objectives can be translated to other projects.

Fort Collins History Connection

The Fort Collins (Colorado) History Connection is a collaborative project between the Fort Collins Museum of Discovery and the Poudre River Public Library District in which the institutions joined together to digitize historical resources from the library and from the museum's archive and artifact collection.

In their early planning stages, they developed a guiding document that identified the vision for the collaboration and major tasks involved and which institution was responsible for them. According to Peggy Shaughnessy, web applications developer for the Poudre River Public Library District, "Mostly we met weekly, communicated well, and planned everything together. The biggest collaboration was during the migration process to a new database for digital collections. First we created criteria and found a product we liked. Next we planned exactly how we wanted the new database to work, cleaned up collections, created standards and controlled vocabularies, invented new workflows, planned website changes, and set up a timeline with assigned responsibilities. Currently, the museum does the data entry and maintenance. I am the systems administrator for the product."

Lesley Struc, curator of the Fort Collins Local History Archive at the museum, notes, "I really recommend carefully documenting everything that's going on while it's happening. I have a large binder of all of our meeting notes, database decisions, and general information that I still refer to."[6]

The Northfield History Collaborative

The Northfield History Collaborative (NHC) occurred when multiple institutions—libraries, historical societies, governmental agencies, cultural organizations, churches, and so on—in the southern Minnesota town of Northfield noticed that local history was scattered throughout various area institutions without a means for sustained coordination and cooperation in making these records accessible.[7] The collaboration operates under a memorandum of understanding between the partners.

In 2007 a group of librarians and archivists in the Northfield area began meeting to address this problem of fragmentation of the historical record by developing a set of relationships, policies, and practices, and an infrastructure to provide a single portal for access to Northfield area history. This founding group created an affiliation that is now known as the NHC. The collaboration's board meets monthly to discuss activities such as digitization standards, workshop planning, furthering grant opportunities, broadening access, and more. The board has even done a work session in which members worked with one of the partner's collections to sort and organize records.

From 2007 to 2011, staff from the four founding organizations—the Northfield Historical Society, the Rice County Historical Society, the Northfield Public Library, and Carleton College—worked together to identify, describe, organize, and provide access to books, manuscripts, photographs, institutional and corporate records, genealogical materials, and other materials relevant to understanding the history of their community and planning for its future. Scanning takes place at the Northfield Historical Society and at Carleton College. The digitized materials are made accessible through a Content DM platform through Carleton College.

Funding from several Minnesota Historical Society grants supported the design and implementation of this initial portal, as well as the digitizing and compilation of pilot collections from each organization. Grant funding also allows for a part-time project manager.

The initial subject scopes were broadly defined as "education in Northfield" and the "1876 attempted bank raid by the James-Younger Gang," so the collection is rich in these materials. Now the subject scope has been broadened to include all types of materials relating to the history of the Northfield area.

In 2011 the membership of the NHC was expanded to include seven additional partners—First National Bank of Northfield, KYMN Radio, Northfield Arts Guild, Northfield Hospital, *Northfield News*, St. John's Lutheran Church, and St. Olaf College. Selected materials from the archives of these organizations are now being added to the portal.

According to Debby Nitz, resource librarian at the Northfield Public Library, "The library was a logical founding partner [of the collaborative] because we have a very strong local history collection and house the only microfilm of the local papers." Your library could be a natural fit for collaboration like this, too.

COLLABORATE—IF IT'S RIGHT FOR YOU

Many of our survey respondents mentioned collaborative projects with which they were involved. Several provided housing for genealogical or other special collections. Others had participated in digitization projects with other local groups. Collaboration can be your best solution when it comes to achieving goals for which you do not have the staff or the finances to fulfill. No doubt there are other librarians just like you trying to achieve similar goals! Reaching out to others via the PLASC discussion list and other means can help you build those relationships.

NOTES

1. Murray Shepherd, *Library Collaboration: What Makes It Work?* Paper presented at the 2004 International Association of University Libraries (IATUL) Conference, Krakow, Poland. www.iatul.org/doclibrary/public/Conf_Proceedings/2004/Murray20Sheperd.pdf.

2. Morten T. Hansen, *Collaboration: How Leaders Avoid the Traps, Create Unity and Reap Big Results* (Boston: Harvard Business Review Press, 2009).
3. Elaine Hayes (Special Collections librarian, Laramie County Library System) interview with Kathy Marquis and Leslie Waggener, July 26, 2012.
4. The PLASC website can be found at www2.archivists.org/groups and contains news and resources related to building and sustaining local history reference collections.
5. Local History Committee, Reference and User Services Association, www.ala .org/rusa/sections/history/committees/localhistory.
6. Lesley Struc (curator, Local History Archive at the Fort Collins [Colorado] Museum of Discovery) interview with Leslie Waggener, October 7, 2014. See http://history.fcgov.com for more information about this collaboration.
7. See http://northfieldhistorycollaborative.org for more information about this collaboration.

| CHAPTER 6 | # FACILITY NEEDS AND PRESERVATION OF LHRC MATERIALS |

Since Pam started as director of the Westview Public Library five years ago, she has noticed repeated requests for materials related to the small town of Westview. Maybe it's time to consider a section for local history in her library. She has some of the items on hand but feels better organization is needed. Right now they're stuffed onto shelves in an unmarked corner of the library. And some staff training would help, herself included! But how to go about creating a distinct place devoted to local history in her modest library? Will she have to collect everything that comes her way in order to create a useful collection? She considers the types of history-related requests she has received over the years. Many were answerable through printed or near-print materials. That sounds more manageable. She decides that an inventory of what the library already has in stock is a good place to start. And a chat with other librarians in her region is a good idea. Maybe this idea isn't impossible after all.

ARE YOU READY to feel relieved? Since we are advising you on how to start a local history reference collection of mostly published materials, we won't be discussing the knottier issues that come with starting an archival collection, such as those we discussed in our chapter on archival versus local history sections. Remember we mentioned that, with archival collections, you need to consider such issues as climate-controlled storage, specialized shelving for archival boxes of various sizes, collection processing, and finding aids? Choosing a local history reference collection means taking a simpler approach. For published materials, your top considerations will be research space, housing the materials, formats, staffing, and equipment needed for access.

SO HOW MUCH ROOM WILL I NEED?

Let's start with research space because, ideally, that area in your library should include materials your patrons will want to look at. As we mentioned in the chapter on collection development, you will want to identify what you already have in your library and pull the items together into one space to create your local history area. The formats you pull together will help determine the size, type, and location of the space you need. Be sure to leave some room for new acquisitions, too. Is your collection mostly books? Do you have or do you want to create vertical files? Need a cabinet for maps? Do you intend to have patrons register before using your local history materials? If so, where and using what criteria? Do you have ephemera that may walk off with an avid patron? Our chapter on reference and access provides some considerations when it comes to registration and security of your materials.

For a research area, you will need at least one table for patron use (see figure 6.1). If you can, provide a computer station since a number of databases used for historical research and genealogy are accessed online. A photocopier may be needed as well, although the main copier in your library can be used if you don't have the space or funds to provide one in your local history space. Consider that many patrons are now using their digital cameras and scanners to make copies. There are also photocopiers that will scan documents for patrons. But a traditional paper copier is more affordable and will still come in handy for patrons.

Do you have microfilm or microfiche in the collection? Your research space could include room for that, or at least an indication of where patrons can go to look at it. However, with the number of online databases, you may find that patrons simply are not looking at microfilm.

If the collection is not separately staffed, and you have rare or unique items in the LHRC, it would be best to place those at the circulation desk for library use only, with an indication of that restriction in the online catalog. If you want to feature new acquisitions or other items, you may want to consider a small exhibit space in the research area to highlight items of interest.

FIGURE 6.1

A separate study area with tables and good observation lines provides comfort for patrons and security for your collections

You may simply not have the room to create a special space for an LHRC. That's okay. If your materials are cataloged as we recommend in the reference and access chapter, discoverability will be keyed in to the online catalog. One of our survey respondents noted that, in his or her public library, "We don't have a separate physical collection, but we do have a digital archive of local history photos."

I HAVE SO MUCH STUFF—HOW DO I HOUSE IT?

Housing for your materials can be simple. For books and booklets, shelf space is your consideration. For small paper-based items, you may want to establish a vertical file system. We talk more about vertical files in our reference and access chapter. If your collection has a number of maps, a map cabinet may be best in order to store the items flat. Otherwise, you can consider a box to hold the maps, with folders indicating the subject of the map(s). Such boxes are available from a number of archival suppliers, such as Gaylord, University Products, and Hollinger Metal Edge. While we discourage collecting objects (or "realia," as they are sometimes called), you may have small collections of ephemera, such as political buttons. For these, a box can also work well. Archival suppliers sell boxes specifically for ephemeral items. Costs are not prohibitive. Sharing an order with a sister library may work for both of you when it comes to ordering boxes of this type.

Where to put these boxes of maps and ephemera? We suggest in-library use only. That could mean putting them behind the circulation desk, or at the reference desk for the LHRC, or in another locked room with access by library staff only. If you are able to provide digital copies on your website, even better for access. Think of linking the catalog record to the digital copy.

BUT I HAVE MATERIALS THAT ARE "ARCHIVAL"

Say you already have materials in your collection that are normally found in an archive, such as photographs, cassette tapes of oral histories, VHS tapes, and more. Do you have the means to care for them in a secure, climate-controlled area with registered access for patrons? Can you digitize them to a more up-to-date and accessible format, perhaps in collaboration with other institutions in your area, such as described in our collaboration chapter? If so, that's great! If you do not have the means to care for these highly fugitive items properly or provide access, deaccessioning the materials to a repository that can better care for them is an option to consider. Remember that you can always put a note in your online catalog that the materials are available at another institution.

You may have a volunteer who will enjoy transcribing the oral history interviews you feel will be of most value to your patrons. Then you can keep a copy of the transcript before deaccessioning the materials. Other archival materials such as personal papers and organizational records may also have a better home at another repository, although you will need to check your donor agreements before weeding. It may be hard to give up those materials, but it's all about getting patrons to the resources and preserving them for future generations. If another repository can do it better then that is something to consider. And remember, the online catalog can provide discoverability as to where those materials are now housed.

If there are archival materials that do belong to your library, such as your library's organizational history, and you want to care for them and provide access, take a look at two resources in particular, Elizabeth Yakel's *Starting* an *Archives* and Faye Phillips's *Local History Collections in Libraries.*[1] Although both resources are dated, they still provide valuable basic information for libraries that house materials considered archival.

RUNNING THE SHOW

We've talked about where to put the materials and how to house them. What about who is going to run the show? A variety of factors can determine staffing needs. These can include preservation issues, acquisition, patron requests both on-site and off-site, and more. Use of volunteers, charging a research fee to non-county residents, staffing the LHRC with a librarian or archivist, and making access to the materials as self-serve as possible are some of the strategies that showed up in our survey. A respondent commented that she is the "archivist, local historian, cataloger, policy writer, & usual buyer, as well as the director of the library," a situation that may sound familiar to a number of our readers.

The choice of how to staff the LHRC depends on the type of collection you provide. In this book, we are describing simple print-based collections. Your LHRC of mostly published materials can be managed by staff and select volunteers in your library once they are at ease with the types of materials you have at hand.

Training staff and volunteers can be a self-service process and need not take hours of your time. In the reference and access chapter, we go over techniques for training staff in use of the LHRC. These same techniques can apply to volunteers. What you're looking for is comfort level. Even if staff or volunteers can't answer a patron's question right away, they can explore the resources with the patron and both can learn. It's about avoiding the deer-in-the-headlights look on the part of staff, volunteers, and patrons.

Discoverability through the online catalog can go a long way to making your LHRC a self-service venture, although not all questions can be answered through the online catalog. Most patrons' grandmothers or grandfathers aren't listed as a specific catalog record (wouldn't that be nice!). You might want to think about a Frequently Asked Questions (FAQ) handout and online link when it comes to the most common requests. The online link can be particularly useful in guiding patrons to databases and digitized materials that will help their research. An FAQ can address hours, location of the LHRC in your library, geographic coverage of your LHRC, policies on making copies (copying delicate materials and use of scanners and digital cameras), services you are able to provide, highlights of your collection, interlibrary loan procedures, reasons for any access limitations (Why is everything not browseable on a shelf?, Why is it not all digitized?, Why do library staff reshelve items instead of having patrons do so?), and more as needed. It can also suggest methods of research ("Start first with what you know! Talk to family members!") and links to other handy guides.

MY LHRC IS FALLING APART AT THE SEAMS

So the books in your LHRC have shattered bindings, the news clippings are yellow and crispy, and the vertical files are—well, they're not yet vertical, but rather limp and lifeless. Now what? Once you have identified the materials for your LHRC, you can identify where the problems lie. See appendix D for an example of a condition form for a damaged item(s). If you have the means, one of the best ways to provide access to delicate materials without having to pull originals is through digitization. However, we realize not everyone has the resources to do so.

Photocopying and disposing of acidic newspaper clippings is one way to deal with that accumulation of yellowed paper. "But I have hundreds of clippings!" you say. Here is where prioritization comes in. Which subjects are being requested most often? Making photocopies is most definitely a volunteer project, and can be a student project as well. If your library has a means of displaying digital content, consider using a digital camera of adequate quality or a scanner to make copies of the clippings, although you may still want to photocopy them as well for longevity. Do not feel as if every clipping has to be copied in a day. Your LHRC is for the long term. Priorities need to be set, and some tracking will need to be done to note your progress.

Delicate and unique books also need tender loving care. Book cradles are one solution for viewing those items without shattering the bindings. The archival suppliers mentioned earlier in this chapter carry such items. Can't afford a book cradle? Try a pillow, such as a couch pillow. What you're looking for is a supportive nest for the book that will not cause it to splay. Never use transparent tape when repairing torn pages in a book, or any paper item. It is acidic and, over time, yellows and loses its adhesiveness. Archival suppliers sell non-acidic tape that is much better suited for repairing pages. Instructions for reattaching or "tipping in" pages torn from a book can be found online and on YouTube. However, if you don't have staff time to do this type of work, consider simply housing the book in a box that fits the book as well as possible, allowing room to remove and replace the book in its enclosure. A book this delicate is one of those items that most likely will not circulate, but will be kept in a restricted section (behind the circulation desk, for example) with a note about the restriction in the online catalog.

If you have photographs in your collection and you choose not to deaccession them to another repository, gloves will be needed when staff or patrons handle them. Oils and acids in the skin eat away at the gelatin in prints and cause smudges. Archival suppliers offer a variety of gloves from washable cotton to disposable nylon. Many local retail stores have cotton gloves too. You can go on the honor system and have gloves in the LHRC for patrons to use with photographs, or issue gloves with photographs if your system of accessing photos is not self-service. We are not going to recommend you provide every photograph with a mylar sleeve, unless you have the means to do so. But you may want to consider sleeving the more valuable photographs. Again, archival suppliers offer mylar sleeves in all sizes.

Another consideration when it comes to photographs is how best to store them. If you have a lot of loose photographs that have no paper documents for context, you may want to have a vertical file system devoted to those photographs. That way they are not mixed up with your other materials and you can better control the handling of them (remember the gloves!). If you have photographs that have contextual material with them, we do not recommend you separate the photographs from that context. If there are paper documents that go with certain photographs, keep the grouping together in your vertical file system.

Ordering special archival boxes and other items such as those listed above is where cooperation with a sister library can come in handy.

WHERE'S THE MONEY?

Establishing an LHRC is most likely where grant money will come in. Maintaining the LHRC will most likely need to be through a more enduring fund. We recommend you become familiar with the State Historical Records Advisory Board (SHRAB) in your state. The SHRAB is the central advisory body for historical records coordination within each state and for the National Historical Publications and Records Commission (NHPRC). All fifty states plus the District of Columbia and Puerto Rico have a SHRAB led by a state coordinator who is the state archivist or someone designated by the state archivist to serve as coordinator. SHRABs have a special relationship with the NHPRC, the grant-making arm of the National Archives and Records Administration. Authorized under NHPRC regulations, SHRABs are responsible for reviewing grant proposals submitted to NHPRC from organizations in their states.

SHRABs also do statewide planning for historical records and often take on additional leadership or coordination roles. A directory of SHRABs can be found on the Council of State Archivists website at www.statearchivists .org/shrabs.htm. Grant opportunities offered by NHPRC can be found on the NHPRC website at www.archives.gov/nhprc.

Another organization to get to know is the Institute of Museum and Library Services (IMLS), which is an independent agency of the U.S. government established in 1996 as a combination of the Institute of Museum Services and the Library Programs Office. IMLS is the main source of federal support for libraries and museums within the United States and offers numerous grants to libraries, museums, and other cultural institutions to support their strategic goal of advancing "innovation, lifelong learning, and cultural and civic engagement." For local history collections, some IMLS grants to note are the Conservation Assessment Program, the National Leadership Grants for Libraries, and, for digitization projects, the Library Services and Technology Act (LSTA) grants. For information about IMLS grants, see their website at www.imls.gov.

The National Endowment for the Humanities (NEH) offers funding that may assist your library, such as the Preservation Assistance Grants for Smaller Institutions, which help libraries and other cultural institutions improve their ability to preserve and care for their humanities-based collections that can include books and journals, archives and manuscripts, prints and photographs, moving images, sound recordings, architectural and cartographic records, decorative and fine art objects, textiles, archaeological and ethnographic artifacts, furniture, historical objects, and digital materials. This is only one of a number of grant offerings by NEH. Check out their website at www.neh .gov for more details.

The Public Library Association (PLA) offers some small grants that could be of help to you. The Upstart Innovation Award, sponsored by Upstart, a Demco company (formerly the Highsmith Library Innovation Award), recognizes a public library's innovative and creative service program to the community.

Some states have agencies or private organizations that may be possible funders. The Paul G. Allen Family Foundation provides grants in the Pacific Northwest area and includes libraries in their funding priorities. In Wyoming, there is the Wyoming Cultural Trust Fund that has the mission to fund projects that protect the state's arts and cultural and historic resources. In Minnesota, the Minnesota Historical Society administers the Historical & Cultural Heritage Grants program. The New Jersey Historical Commission offers General Operating Support Grants, project grants, and mini-grants to support a variety of programs and activities related to New Jersey history.

It also offers prizes and free archival evaluation services through the Caucus Archival Projects Evaluation Service, or CAPES. Guidelines for the grants and prizes program (along with reporting requirements for grant recipients) are available on the New Jersey State Library website. When looking for these types of state-based grants, a good place to start is with your state archives or state library. They may know of local or regional funding sources for historical projects.

Do you have a benefactor in the community who has the means to help you and just needs to be asked? A donation of this type can come as an immediate gift or as a planned gift. If your library has a foundation staff, you could let them know of the potential donor and work with the staff on preparing for the ask. But you may not have the benefit of a foundation. We know—when it comes to asking for donations, many of us head for the hills. However, as any professional fund-raiser knows, at its heart fund-raising is helping others connect an existing passion directly to your cause. An online document provided by NonprofitHub.org titled "7 Tips on Asking for Donations" lists basic techniques for approaching a donor for funds.[2] These include:

1. Research your potential donor (the web is great for this).

2. Make it clear in your *first* contact that you're interested in talking to them about your cause and how they might be able to get involved. In other words, don't surprise them.

3. Don't be scared of sounding weird or too forward by asking things like, "What do you think is the biggest challenge we face in this area?" Provoke interesting reactions that are memorable, not boring, formulaic encounters.

4. Ask for advice. The donor may freely tell you the secret thing they are most passionate about, as well as their biggest fears about giving. So ask for their input and impressions.

5. Don't always fill the silence; use strategic silence. Journalists love this technique—it gets them the best interviews and quotes. You too can use this tool and let the donor speak.

6. Ask for a specific amount (don't make your donor do any work).

7. Practice the ask—and practice again.

Founder of FundraisingCoach.com Marc Pitman suggests two possible phrases to use when asking a donor for funds: "Would you consider a gift of $____?" and "Honestly, I have *NO* idea how much to ask you for, but is a gift of $____ something you'd be able to consider?"[3] You might be surprised when your donor gives you an enthusiastic "YES!" to your request for funds. But don't be discouraged if it doesn't happen right away. Part of this type of work is building relationships that last. And remember that your library's Friends group is also part of your donor base. Make sure they know your purpose, how your LHRC benefits the library and the community, and how much you need to fund your LHRC. Just be sure to work with your library's director, who may have other ideas about funding the library needs from your Friends.

■ ■ ■

As you can see, starting a local history reference collection of mostly published materials does not have to be a daunting prospect. The library may already have many of the materials you need at hand. It's just a matter of pulling it together. Remember that most likely there are others who care about the community's history—think of them as collaborators, volunteers, and donors, in terms of both materials and funds!

NOTES

1. Elizabeth Yakel, *Starting an Archives* (Society of American Archivists, 1994). An updated version of *Local History Collections in Libraries* (Libraries Unlimited, 1995) by Faye Phillips is forthcoming.
2. Marc Koenig, "7 Tips on Asking for Donations—It's Intimidating, We Get It," *Nonprofit Hub,* 2013, www.nonprofithub.org/fundraising/7-tips-on -asking-for-donations-its-intimidating-we-get-it.
3. Marc Pitman, "2 Phrases to Use When Asking for Money," 2012, http:// fundraisingcoach.com/2012/05/08/2-phrases-to-use-when-asking-for-money.

CHAPTER 7 | # REFERENCE AND ACCESS

"Monica, do you have a minute? There's a couple who want help using our local history room, and I'm really not sure what to tell them . . ." Monica looks up to see the new reference librarian, Sonya, looking nervously at her. Why is Sonya so uncomfortable with this collection? She has years of reference experience elsewhere. What is it about genealogy questions that makes everyone doubt their skills at helping patrons? Monica gets up to lend a hand, but vows to begin additional training with her staff to make sure everyone is comfortable discovering what patrons want and to help them find their answers.

PROVIDING ACCESS TO your LHRC is certainly a logical extension of the assistance you provide to patrons everywhere in your library. But how is it unlike reference for other parts of a library's collection? And on the other hand, how could it be in sync with other library services instead of making it unnecessarily complicated by reinventing the wheel?

In this chapter we will discuss several aspects of access: How do patrons discover what you have? What barriers do they experience in using historical sources? Do barriers include bewilderment about these sources on the part of library staff members like Sonya? How can we help patrons and staff understand local history sources—many of which can be difficult to use? And, what types of access policies should you set to protect your materials?

Using historical materials can often be more challenging than using the rest of your library's collection. If your reference staff is having difficulty figuring out how to make sense of it, how much more confusing must your public find these materials? LHRCs are often in a separate room, sometimes with different rules for when and how materials can be accessed. Sometimes you refer to it as a "special" collection and its users as "researchers." And, often, the items in the LHRC aren't included in the library's main catalog. Get the picture?

"I DIDN'T KNOW YOU HAD THAT!"

The primary reason to collect local history materials is so that our patrons can use them. In order to do that, they must first learn that the materials exist and that they are available at your library. How are they likely to do that? The key concept here is "discoverability": how easy is it for anyone to find out what is in your library? Throughout this section we will be asking "What do patrons need to do or know to find out what you have? How many steps do they need to take? Have you followed the simplest path to discovery by using the fewest number of places where they must search?"

Let's start with the most basic point of access: the library catalog. If patrons are familiar with using the catalog to find out what you have on a particular topic, they will probably assume that this applies to your local history materials, too. If someone is looking for information on the First Lutheran Church, shouldn't its anniversary volume, even if it is in the LHRC, be discoverable in your online catalog? What about clippings relating to the church? Are the headings for your vertical file (or whatever it might be called) also entered into the catalog? If the answer on either count is "no," we encourage you to talk to your technical services department about intellectually integrating local history materials, including descriptions in the library's catalog. Many libraries already handle collections this way (if that helps in your negotiations). Ultimately, this is a service to patrons. Don't ask library staff to learn separate access systems for historical research that they will not be able to use for other types of library work. Use what they already know.

LHRCs often contain a cascading set of smaller and smaller collections, each with its own inherent organization scheme. At the top are the published volumes. Cataloging these into the library's collection should not pose too many problems, as they conform to the standards of the library collections. The catch may be that many are older, unique, the only surviving copies, or otherwise not the simple copy cataloging task of your library's best sellers. If you have time and an interest, you might offer to assist the technical services department in researching the authority information necessary to enter these items into your catalog. Keep in mind that your library may also have circulating copies of some of these items, so that will make adding the LHRC copies that much easier.

The next level is the non-monograph published items: local serials, newspapers, and newsletters. These, too, should have title-level entries in the catalog and be checked in as you would other serial publications. The difference is that you will keep a full back file of issues, unless they are preserved on microfilm or available digitally from a library, not just from the publisher of the serial, which could stop providing access to them. You won't weed them after a year or two as you would issues of *Time* or *People*.

One special note on historical newspapers: we have encountered quite a bit of interest on the part of public librarians in starting special projects to digitize copies of local newspapers. Before you begin such a project—or seek funding to do it—please consult your state archives and/or state library. Many states have already undertaken massive newspaper microfilming and/or digitization projects of which you may be unaware. All you have to do is purchase the microfilm reels, or in many cases, link to the digitized files on your library's catalog or website. Easy! An excellent place to start is this list of historical newspapers online, compiled by the librarians at the University of Pennsylvania: http://viewshare.org/views/refhelp. Save all that energy for items that have not already been preserved!

Following this are the informally published or ephemeral items: the pamphlets, clippings, photocopies, and other print items that help you document your local area. How do you keep them? We strongly recommend creating one ephemeral or vertical file. If you can, make a practice of photocopying clippings and other highly acidic items (think newsprint or manila paper—old and yellowing) onto regular photocopy paper. This is a great job for a regular volunteer—one who can understand the tricks of your library's photocopier so that the copies are readable and all sections of a story are included.

Hanging files are useful for this type of collection. And here's the "don't reinvent the wheel" advice you saw coming: make the folder headings conform to Library of Congress subject headings (or whatever subject headings you already use in your online catalog), and include them in the catalog, too (see figure 7.1). A win for discoverability! Finding such a heading in the catalog should prompt the patron to ask where the file is and thus give you a chance to promote the LHRC.

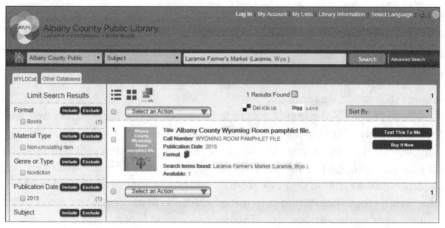

FIGURE 7.1

Vertical file record in the library catalog

Courtesy of the Wyoming State Library

The final level is the special materials like bound clippings, oral history interviews (if you have them), family trees, and other compilations that seem to beg us to put them in separate locations, leave them out of catalogs, arrange them in unique ways, and otherwise make them opaque and unusable by our patrons. What to do about them?

There is no reason not to catalog these items, too. They will add to the original cataloging burden of your technical services department, so keep that in mind when you are advocating for this, if it is a change for your library. It is important to remind your administration that if these items are not cataloged, they can be completely invisible both to your patrons and to the staff you hope will promote their use. Some of these items have separate indices. If the index constitutes a separate item, catalog it. If not, be sure to note the presence of the index in the catalog record. These indices and lists are the last, hidden level of your collection and one that your staff should promote to make the collection most usable to your patrons.

We were very pleased to discover that more than 75 percent of the respondents to our survey already include many of their LHRC materials in their main library catalog. But a significant minority, even some of those who said they cataloged their LHRC materials, revealed that they also have separate finding systems for those "special" portions of their collections, the vertical files, photographs, scrapbooks, unpublished family histories, maps, and "artifacts and memorabilia." One survey respondent explained how her system works, "Published books are organized by Dewey decimal numbers that are separate from the standard catalog. The call numbers are organized in a binder. Photographs are organized by number. Classification systems are being devised for the vertical files and maps collections." Another respondent added, ruefully, "Our monographs are in our Catalog, the vertical file and some ephemera have print finding aids, the photos are in ContentDM and we have Newspaper microfilm with some print indexes. A mixed bag to be sure!" Others have created separate Google Docs, Access databases, Excel spreadsheets, paper subject guides, or lists in binders. We argue that these add-on systems complicate access for patrons and library staff.

It appears that books are a no-brainer: we naturally put them in the catalog. But when "special" materials are also included, the temptation to create special lists and descriptions takes over. For many libraries, these take the form of specially created databases, searchable only via the library's website. Others are purchasing separate cataloging software such as PastPerfect, a museum artifact cataloging system, to manage ephemera, oral histories, and other materials. In both cases, the temptation to describe at the item level can make a straightforward task into a labor-intensive backlog. The irony is that cataloging conventions already exist for these materials, which can then be easily included in the main library catalog, using Library of Congress descriptors and OCLC rules. Although we are not emphasizing unpublished materials in this book, if you have that type of material and want to hang on to it or acquire it, then consider including it in the main library catalog.

HOW DO I CATALOG THIS STUFF?

What librarians with these small but special collections may not realize is that the tried-and-true MARC 21 format—the same one the technical processing department is already using for monographs and serials—works just as well for unpublished and near-print materials. In fact, it is that same MARC format that archivists across the country already use for catalog-level records for their manuscript and archival collections. The answer was right there all along!

What is the advantage of integrating these records into your library catalog? Discoverability! Local history materials come up in a regular catalog search along with books and other materials in the main collection with no need to look in a separate list or database. It's actually the best way to promote your collection because patrons find citations to materials as part of what matters most to them: their search for their own research topic. (See figure 7.2.)

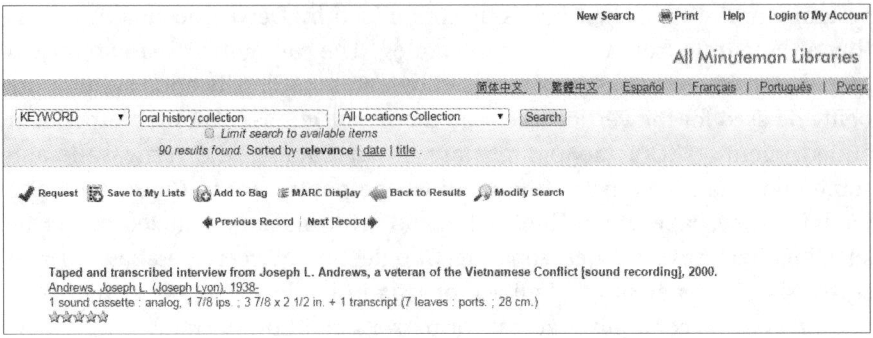

FIGURE 7.2

**Oral history record in the Minuteman
(Massachusetts) Public Library catalog**

Courtesy of the Minuteman Library Network, Natick, Massachusetts

A significant stumbling block is that using systems separate from your online catalog involves original, not copy, cataloging. This may not be a regular practice for many technical service librarians who are accustomed to finding existing records online and downloading them to their catalogs. As one survey respondent lamented, "We do not have [an] original cataloger on staff and we have tons of ephemera."

WHAT'S IN THAT ROOM?

The next barrier, or discomfort level, concerns the physical location of your local history reference collection. LHRCs come in all shapes, sizes, parts of the library, and ways in which they are found. Ninety percent of our survey respondents said that their local history materials are in some separate area, not on the open shelves. Three quarters of these collections are open whenever the library is, and over half have no special staffing—all reference staff assist patrons there. Just the fact that you have given the local history reference collection a separate name or space could make patrons wonder if they are allowed to use it.

What are some of the other ways we may be inadvertently keeping patrons from using our collections—even as we establish guidelines to preserve these collections for future users? If you are just establishing an LHRC, here are basic questions to ask. If the LHRC already exists, ask yourself anyway and think how your answers affect patrons' ease of access.

- Are local historical materials shelved with the rest of your collection?
- Are they separately shelved but accessible to the general public with no intermediary staff?
- Are they in a separate room?
- Are they part of the circulating collection, or are they "in-library use only"?
- Does the LHRC have fewer open hours than the rest of the library?
- Is there a registration process for using the collection?
- Are LHRC patrons asked to put bags and pens aside or in lockers?
- Are patrons' bags searched when exiting the LHRC?
- Is self-service copying of LHRC materials allowed?

There are many sound reasons for requiring registration of patrons, asking them to put away their bags and pens, making the collection non-circulating, and keeping the collection in a separate, even locked and separately staffed area. Most of these reasons have to do with security. If the items in this area are unique—irreplaceable—it is preferable that they not circulate and that staff monitor the collection's use. Many libraries can't afford to separately staff their LHRC, but they may be able to train volunteers to do this (the local genealogical society could provide a pool of such volunteers, for example). How you organize your LHRC will vary with your library's level of commitment to the collection, its size and use potential, and budgetary realities. At the very least, it will be helpful to have this collection in close proximity to a staffed reference desk with direct sight lines into the collection's stacks and user area. This will increase the ability to monitor traffic, exercise preventive security by making it less easy to steal or damage materials, and encourage patrons to seek your research assistance.

Nonetheless, all of these security measures can have a dampening effect on patrons' willingness to cross over the threshold and explore your carefully constructed collection. The hours may not coincide with their free time. The rules may seem formidable. They may just walk by the room or alcove and never go in, not realizing it has information they can use.

Many of these obstacles can be addressed by techniques we discuss in our chapter on marketing. Others can be overcome by digitizing highly used materials and making them available outside the walls of your library, on your patrons' timetable. The others constitute an internal barrier that we consider next.

"I DON'T KNOW HOW TO USE THAT STUFF"

As we've seen, this can apply to your staff, as well as your patrons. Psychological barriers to using research collections are real. Patrons want to find out information from your collection. But they also have a desire to appear knowledgeable, to not feel unwelcome or out of place—in other words, not to feel dumb. This can be true anywhere in your library—think of how many patrons have no idea how to use the library catalog or the Dewey Decimal System to find a book. It is compounded in your LHRC by even less familiarity with the sources, and how they may look or be organized. All your public service skills, and especially your ability to empathize, will come in handy in these reference interactions.

If this level of discomfort seems unlikely to you, take a minute to think about a place that you would hesitate to enter because you don't understand how it's organized or how to use what is there. For some, it might be a home improvement store (What are all those gadgets? Do I need to know how to use them to attempt my project?) For others it might be a gym (Which equipment do I need? How do I adjust the settings? Are there time limits on them that I don't know about?). Natural insecurities like these make it easy to decide that you can't use those materials, you wouldn't understand them, you probably need special instruction, and so on. Best to give it a miss.

If your LHRC has its own dedicated staff or volunteers, they can help bridge these gaps in comfort level by being extra welcoming, displaying encouraging signage, giving public classes, and so on. If your LHRC is unstaffed, brochures in the rest of the library encouraging use will be helpful, as will tutorials or libguides that can help educate patrons. They can discover these aids on their own, or you can point them out as you offer assistance. Either way, staff should be ready to give extra hand-holding with these materials. And they should promote use of the local history reference collection when handling other reference requests, when a question reveals that the LHRC is the place to find more information.

"MAY I HELP YOU?"

What kind of staff training is useful for your local history reference collection? In many cases you can assume that your staff's level of comfort and expertise is not much different than that of your patrons. However, you will expect your staff to teach the public how to use your collection—and make them feel comfortable. Give staff the tools they'll need to get patrons started on their search so that you, or other more experienced researchers, can answer more complex questions. Remind staff that their lack of familiarity with the sources may be mirrored in every patron they assist. Make sure they understand that their help includes empathy as well as education. They should be communicating that the search can be fun and rewarding—and possible to do—and that staff are glad to answer questions.

Begin staff training with a very brief overview of the strengths and coverage of the collection: is it focused on just your community? A broader region? The next step will be to get them working with the most commonly used items. If your newspapers are the most used feature, give staff lots of practice questions, make sure they are comfortable with your microfilm reading/copying equipment, and ensure they know searching techniques with your online databases, and so on. Have them start by looking up their own birthday or that of their parents. It works with packs of squirmy Cub Scouts and it can work with your staff, too! It gives them a connection to the content and a reason to overcome their hesitance about the format or age of the resource. Make them dig in. Encourage them to look at the ads ("Look how much you could buy a car for in 1928!"). If the most revealing source in your collection is the set of local city directories, have them look up who used to live in their house over several decades. If you have volunteers staffing your LHRC, consider the same training. Don't assume they're experts, unless they've already proven to be so. See appendix E for a handy staff training worksheet that coauthor Kathy used at her library.

Don't forget the census returns. They may not be "in" your LHRC, but it's important to see them as part of it. You are most likely to have access to these via an online database subscription. Make sure your staff understands how to find names, access blank forms for patrons to fill in (also part of the database resources), decipher abbreviations and handwriting, and especially how to encourage patrons to record *where* they found pieces of information. The census may be the only place that a patron's ancestor's name will actually appear. Even the old city directories list mainly "heads of household," which means males. The census recorded all members of the household. Often with family history research, you are going for the "quick win." You want your patrons to find something of meaning to their search. This good result will encourage them to keep looking through other resources, even if those sources have less information on their specific quarry. Again, it's about building comfort and confidence so that they will keep coming back to research. Family history can be a long slog (or, better yet, a treasure hunt). Make it seem worth the effort. When training staff, encourage them to spend work time looking up their own family. It is a great way to encourage them to do the "playing" with the materials that will build their confidence and lead them to ask questions you may not have thought to answer. It may even be the most enjoyable library training they receive.

Your LHRC can also be a gateway to the local genealogical society. Such groups regularly share information between members and do their own hand-holding and confidence building. Make sure patrons can discover these groups via your collection.

There are many excellent guides about researching family and local history. If any have been written with your area in mind, or focus on nationalities common in your area, be sure to collect those publications (print or near-print) for your collection. Your staff, especially if they provide reference for other library areas, will probably only learn the rudiments of family history research techniques. Make sure they are familiar with some of the basic guidelines for starting a search:

> Start with what you know and work backward in time. Don't look for your Pilgrim ancestor first—start by confirming that you know the dates and places associated with your grandparents, then go back another generation and so on.

> Be sure to check with family members to see what they already know. This may seem overly simplistic, but many patrons spend hours, or years, searching for dates and names that an elderly relative could have told them in a moment.

> Suggest that all sources be cited in some central notebook or online file. There's nothing like finding a controversial birth date and, if questioned, having no idea where you found that piece of information.

One last note about the staff you *don't* supervise elsewhere in your building. Invite them into the LHRC periodically for a brief training, or just a little hands-on exploration of the materials. Your goal is that these staff members make accurate—and frequent—referrals to your LHRC, because they understand its value and want to see it used. This type of "in-reach" to your colleagues will also help them understand why some materials require special handling, processing, or security.

FEATURING THE FUN FACTOR

So far, we've focused on overcoming hurdles involved in all the differences inherent in your LHRC. You've thought about the unusual materials, separate setting or hours, possible rules, and special handling. Once you feel that these issues have been satisfactorily addressed with your staff and patrons, providing service for the rest of this collection is familiar territory. You know how to conduct a good reference interview to discover what patrons really want. You are accustomed to determining if a user is embarking on a major project or search, or just needs one source for a quick answer. You know that a fifth grader will need simpler sources and more assistance than a visiting genealogist who's been researching her family for years. You may also want to think of some of the approaches in our chapter on the virtual local history reference collection as a means of promoting self-service to the materials.

Ultimately, the fun factor in the local history reference collection should be high. The "stuff" is old and contains interesting facts, images, and a window into the area's history. The job for you and your staff is to make the materials easy to locate and easy to use. You will need to think about how to balance this ease of use with a need to secure materials that are older and probably not possible to replace. Once you strike that balance, this collection can be a special one, indeed, and a well-used one.

CHAPTER 8

MARKETING AND OUTREACH

"Savannah, are you interested in being an official contributor to our Facebook page? We could use some fresh ideas. Would you be willing to post once a week?" Would she?? Savannah has been dying to show the library's Facebook patrons some of the cool things she has discovered since beginning her job in the library's History Room. When she applied for this job, she especially liked that the library seemed keen to participate in social media. But since learning more about the contents of the History Room, she realizes that what is being showcased on the website and social media is really just the tip of the iceberg in terms of what her room has to offer. She could start with some of the great maps and advertisements in the older city directories. And the stories in the newspapers . . . Some of them are so funny! She is also excited about the possibility of starting a local history club, and she knows that she needs access to public relations to make it happen. Well, best to start with a few things and see how people respond. But the possibilities!

YOU'VE ACCUMULATED A set of interesting and useful local history materials. Letting patrons, both existing and potential, know about them is essential to the relevance of the collection. Of course, cataloging the materials and

FIGURE 8.1

Wilson County (North Carolina) Public Library event poster

The image in this poster is from a World War II U.S. War Production Co-Ordinating Committee educational poster. As a federal document, it is in the public domain. Images from the National Archives are a wonderful source of images that are not under copyright.

Courtesy of Will Robinson, local history and genealogy librarian, Wilson County Public Library

placing them in the library's online catalog is of prime importance, but that is only the first step. Getting the word out to general and specialized audiences is also crucial. A favorite marketing example that came out of our survey was this response: "We do a lot of outreach visits to reach people in 'surprising' places, such as present at a recent Funk parade celebrating local music and have a local author who wrote about beer give a talk at a bar . . . We do significant outreach to the branch library system of 26 locations so staff there will be knowledgeable ambassadors for the collections." You may have those "surprising" places in your own community, and you may have potential "ambassadors" as well. Think of fun ways to advertise the collection, such as the eye-catching poster in figure 8.1.

In this chapter we share some marketing and outreach possibilities. Don't overwhelm yourself by attempting each one, unless you have the staff and resources to do so. Consider using those that work well with existing programs and build from there. An enhanced array of options awaits you, thanks to the addition of social media opportunities. Some methods lend themselves to an approach everyone can appreciate. Let's look at those methods first, and then get down to reaching specific groups, including those that can help your local history reference collection beyond a research capacity. Our chapter on audience and users offers in-depth explanations on the most likely users for your collection.

A BROAD STROKE

Before getting into the particular approaches, there are some fundamentals that feed each one. Think photos! And, if possible, video. Create a photo database so you can keep those photos handy and organized, and always have the digital camera (with fresh batteries) and camcorder (charged and ready) on hand. Nowadays, all you may need is a smartphone to do the work. Put photo consent forms near them. Images can be used in many different ways to advertise the LHRC and enliven textual information. And don't just keep a photo database; also think about a database of personal anecdotes from a multiplicity of patrons that describe how the LHRC has helped in their research. Just a couple of lines from each patron are necessary. These short testimonials can be powerful proof to library administrators, funders, and others that your local history reference collection has value to the community. Think about all the different ways to present information about your collection, be in tune to what is happening at the library and how local history materials might fit in, and be prepared to capture the images, stories, and information that reflect your collection's value. Be proactive in your plans! For example, what are the commemorative months both nationally and locally, and how can you parlay your local history resources into inspiration for a grade school or high school class paper, a History Day project, a historic preservation endeavor, or a local historian's description of the event being commemorated?

BROCHURES—SIMPLE YET ELEGANT (OR NOT)

One of the most basic and wide-reaching methods of marketing your LHRC is through a brochure. Brochures can be everywhere you want them to be—in a stand at the library's circulation desk, handed out at presentations, and mailed with other information to the media and to existing or potential researchers.
Here are basic steps in creating a brochure:

> Compile information, both topical and detailed, about your LHRC. Think of its strong points and highlight them.

> Create a basic framework. Some computer software, such as Microsoft Publisher, already has a variety of templates that make it easy for a brochure to pop out at your audience.

> Think powerful! The front of the brochure should have the name of your LHRC and your library, but keep it basic. No large panels of text here. An eye-catching photo can do wonders for impact.

On the interior, be sure to have clear headings. Lists, bullet points, and testimonials are all successful ways of communicating the significance of your collection.

The back panel should include contact information, as well as the website URL and location information.

Test a draft of the brochure on family, friends, and patrons. Ask them if anything is confusing and whether they feel motivated to come in for a look at the local history materials. While this audience may not offer you specific revisions, their opinions on the overall effectiveness can help you decide if changes are necessary.

Take your brochures to the local genealogy society and Family History Center—and offer to display their brochures in return. It's important that they—and your patrons—realize that all of the organizations in the area that care about the community's history are cooperating—not competing—with each other for the patrons' benefit.

BUILDING YOUR LOCAL HISTORY WEBSITE

Most likely your library has an existing website. Adding a page describing local history materials is a great way to reach a general audience. If you want to create a website specifically for the local history reference collection and are looking for a platform, some open source options are WordPress.com and Drupal (if you have more expertise). Do an online search to explore further options. There are many out there, and more are being established all the time. A number of them are either free or low cost for a basic package.

Fundamental information to include on the website is staff contacts, hours, and guidance on how and where to access the LHRC. Using less formal language to explain the rules can make you sound less forbidding and more welcoming. For example, instead of saying, "No food or drink," add a little blurb as to why, such as, "We're protecting [our town's, city's, region's] history for years to come. Help us out by not consuming food or drink while handling local history materials." Highlight the fact that your local history materials are in the online catalog. Think supportively! Will other history institutions in the community and region put your link on their websites if you'll do the same for them? What is their website content? Can you collaborate? You may be tempted to add link after link of resources for your patrons, but keep in mind that more than ten links on a page can seem overwhelming to viewers. And then there's that important website adage—update it. How often? The short answer is "as often as there is anything worth updating!" The problem is deciding what is worth updating. It will seem like you always have news—recent acquisitions, staff changes, upcoming events, tips—the list goes on. You have things to talk about! You should really make a point to update something on your website once a week or, if that's not possible due to lack of staffing, try once a month. Go through your website on a regular basis to see if there are outdated announcements to remove.

Want to know the website's traffic patterns? Google Analytics is one of the tools you can use. It is a service offered by Google that generates detailed statistics about a website's traffic and traffic sources. The basic service is free, with a premium version available for a fee. Google Analytics can track visitors from all referrers, including search engines and social networks, direct visits, and referring sites. Based on what you find with a service like Google Analytics, you can know what people are searching for on your website. What search terms are patrons using? Are they floundering? Based on what you find, you can make certain aspects of your website more prominent and, if needed, more explanatory.

There is no need to overwhelm yourself with potential content on the local history website. Your web presence can be as extensive as time and resources allow. If you want to go so far as to create a channel for video content, with just a Google account you can create a YouTube channel and upload videos, provide for viewer comments, or make playlists. Remember that you can always start simple and build up. At least create enough content to relay the variety of materials in your collection and to spark interest in its use. In our chapter on the virtual Local History Reference Collection, we will talk more about what you might include on your website.

INVITE A REPORTER TO LUNCH

Have you thought about using the media to get the word out about your collection and its activities? It can be an extremely effective outreach tool. The relationship can be mutually beneficial: the media can use local history materials to help with historical pieces, back stories, and filler on slow news days. Librarians need the media to promote their activities. Reporters typically need information on very short notice, so it will be important to decide how much assistance you can afford to give them. But, whether you will do their research or just guide them in using collection materials, you will be surprised how little they know of what you have.

When contacting a journalist, have several stories ready to pitch and be able to get to the point quickly. Also, be savvy with media deadlines and best contacts at the media outlet. Think about whom at your library should have permission to speak with the media. General inquiries such as hours, policies, and activities could be handled by any staff member, but for more sensitive topics, it is important to determine who should answer the questions.

Consider distributing a short handout to media outlets listing your most useful sources, your hours and contact information, your copying policies, and the services you provide. Use real examples so they can see how LHRC materials can add depth to their stories: older clippings and pamphlets on the mall that is about to be torn down, maps that show how small your growing town once was, local histories listing persons for whom the streets and schools were named—you have it all!

In turn, reporters can help get the word out to potential patrons, and show administrators and library board members that there is enough interest in your LHRC to inspire a news article. Speaking of board members, the authors came across a 1926 national survey of public librarians that mentioned a library board trustee in Trenton, New Jersey, who wrote a regular newspaper column featuring the local history collection.[1] Got any takers on your own library board?

If you can encourage reporters to cite you as a source, their readers will be more likely to seek you out for similar inquiries. Every journalist who is producing a report on a local site, organization, enterprise, or cause will probably want to include a brief historical overview in their introduction. Where will they find out the history of their subject? From you! You may have a pamphlet in your vertical file that gives them everything they need in one place. Or they may have to do a bit of digging in your collection. If so, ask if you can have a copy of what they write so the next person can benefit from their work. Also, you can most likely parlay their use of the collection and their findings into various outlets such as a blog post, newsletter article, and more.

Here are some tips relating to the most common media outlets: television, radio, and newspaper. Much of this information is based on the Society of American Archivists' publication *Public Relations and Marketing for Archives* (2011).[2] Although written for the archival community, the advice provided translates well for libraries housing local history reference collections.

TELEVISION

Some TV stations have special projects or features editors who can be great contacts. Otherwise, assistant news directors, executive producers, or managing editors normally have time to plan stories for weeks or months before going on air; these individuals can be powerful allies and great assets. Develop ideas into news stories by asking the following questions:

- Why is it news? What is "new" about it?
- Who will it affect?
- Why should the viewing audience care?
- Is there a link between your story and a larger news story?
- Are there images to enhance the story?

If being on camera makes you nervous, don't go on; a message delivered by someone who obviously lacks confidence on the air will suffer as a result. Focus the story on patrons who are using the collection. If you have not yet found a patron base, mention specific ways the collection can be useful to potential audiences.

RADIO

No matter what the radio station's objectives, disc jockeys are always looking for interesting stories to attract listeners, and the Federal Communications Commission mandates that each radio station devote a certain number of minutes to public service announcements. Think about creating a template for a public service announcement and adjust as needed. That way you're not inventing it from scratch each time. Also consider an underwriting announcement with the local Public Broadcasting System (PBS) station to advertise your LHRC. Many in the scholarly community are PBS listeners. Underwriting helps financially support PBS stations, which can help build a solid relationship with your local station. If you do a live radio broadcast, know the subjects and try to anticipate any questions that may be asked. Be aware that a taped interview will be edited.

PRINT MEDIA

Cultivate a relationship with a reporter at your local newspaper. Test the waters to see who might be willing to work with you on stories to advertise the LHRC and things that come up regarding it, such as programming and interesting acquisitions. Let the reporter know that you can assist with fact checking or finding interesting information to include in a story. If reporters know they can count on you for help on a backstory, they will be more likely to respond to a request for PR from you.

Learn the template they prefer for press releases. This will get your story noticed and make it easier for news staff to more quickly insert it into the paper. Make sure your press release, or column, begins with the most important information, as a number of readers will not finish the entire piece. Ask patrons and colleagues what they find interesting in the LHRC and use this information to create a story.

HOW TO BE WELL "LIKED"

A social media presence is no longer a choice for libraries; today it is a necessity to remain relevant. Social media tools can let an entirely new audience know about your local history reference collection. Twitter, Facebook, blogging (discussed in more detail later in this chapter), Flickr, Tumblr, YouTube, Historypin, Pinterest, and Google Hangouts (think virtual author visits) are all tools that can be useful to you. One thing to remember is the limits of time and staff resources before deciding which forms of social media to use. Consider creating a publishing schedule for the social media tools you decide to use, such as blogs, Facebook, and Twitter. That way you can be consistent in getting out your content.

Chances are your library is already using several forms of social media. Talk to the PR staff (if you have one) to find out what they want. Ask if you can be added to a rotation of who posts for the library. Excerpts from old newspapers are always entertaining (and informative). Just keep in mind that copyright still applies. Check out Cornell University's chart for when works pass into the public domain at http://copyright.cornell.edu/resources/publicdomain.cfm, or the libguide version in our book, appendix F. Want comments? Try running an advertisement for a new home, from 1920! Can you believe how little it cost to buy a house? Of course, you can also use the fun stuff to highlight the research potential of your collection.

Contributing to a Facebook profile is one of the easiest ways to begin building a social media presence. If your library has a Facebook page, remember that the LHRC is full of interesting content to populate that page, and also other social media. Just keep in mind that the posts should be lively, brief, and informative and should invite comments. Try to avoid simply telling your audience that you have a new item in the collection. Think of something particularly fun or interesting to grab their attention. Ask for polls with questions like "What is your favorite place in the community? What is your favorite history resource?" Put a picture of a card catalog up and ask how many people are old enough to have used it. With social media, many libraries focus on what the library is doing. What are the patrons doing? Most people will "like" a library page in hopes of being informed of current happenings or entertained. If your posts just clog up their ongoing feed with updates on new acquisitions, you will quickly find yourself "unliked" or hidden. Highlighting a patron's project is a great way to thank users—and encourage them to donate finished projects for the collection!

DARE TO BLOG

We give blogs special attention in this chapter due to their effectiveness in telling the story of your LHRC in a personalized, intimate style. Instructions for setting up a blog can be found in sources such as the various "23 Things" websites (starting with the first Learning 2.0 site: http://plcmc12-things.blogspot .com/). If you haven't tried one of these programs, they are an excellent, self-paced way to discover all sorts of social media options. Decide early who will have editorial authority over the blog. Your library may have existing policies that you will need to consider, such as content review by library administrators and privacy issues relating to patron use of library materials. Consider too that those beyond your ideal audience will be able to find what has been written, including funders, other libraries, and your own library's staff.

Don't worry if you don't get the blog right immediately—it may take a number of tries before you hit on the right mix of tone and promotion. Typically a blog highlights exhibits, events and programming, new items, or recent research, but you can also get creative. Does your collection contain a funny photo that just begs for an equally funny caption? Think about a contest for the best description (just make sure it's not a photo of someone's relative). The collection is probably full of interesting and fun trivia about your community. Blog about it!

Blogging once a week is a good baseline; if you go more than a month between updates, it will look like the blog is no longer used. Are there others at your library you can tap for blog posts about local history and the collection? Creating a rotating responsibility for updates can be useful to keep content fresh. What about asking a collection researcher to write a quick post? A middle school or high school History Day student using your collection could create an appealing post for a younger audience. Mix up content, images, and other media as you can. Remember, you're not necessarily writing for an academic audience, so stay away from long dense blocks of text, but keep spelling and grammar in mind. The blog may be informal, but it's still no place to be sloppy.

Will you allow viewers' comments? All blogging software includes several options for comments—allowed, moderated, or closed (none allowed). Comments sections allow for interesting discussion, but spam can be a problem. You could start out with "free" comments and switch later to moderating or even closing comments. Whether your library allows comments will depend on the library's goals for the blog, as well as other policies, workflow, and (later) traffic.

How do you know if your blog is being read? There are a number of free tools and resources that can help you analyze the blog's popularity and what users are searching for. You can use the information to help you decide future content and to make decisions about what part of your LHRC to highlight. Google Analytics is one option to consider; StatCounter is another. Both tools are free and provide reports such as visitor paths, popular pages, search terms, and maps of where visitors are coming from. Be sure to encourage readers to subscribe to your blog through RSS feeds so they are notified every time you post a new entry.

ENTICING SPECIFIC USERS

Choosing one group of people that you fully understand in terms of what they value, how they use your resources, and what their outcomes are can be one of the best ways to achieve quick results from marketing. Let's think of them as your guinea pigs. According to library strategic marketing guru Terry Kendrick, quick wins feed the excitement of library staff to continue with marketing efforts. Kendrick explains, "There's a phrase about how you can lead a horse to water but you can't make it drink. The real trick is to make the horse thirsty, then take it to the water. To make people thirsty for marketing within your organization, you have to show them quick wins, because in these difficult times no one wants to work hard on something that won't bear fruit for three to five years. There are a lot of benefits in the long-term view, but it takes a lot of nerve to just wait for them. So you need the quick wins to help get you there."[3] Here are some tools to consider when communicating to a target audience about the usefulness of your LHRC. Pick and choose the tools you find useful and doable for your library.

NEWSLETTERS

A newsletter is a great way to serve a particular audience and bring positive attention by that group to the LHRC. The first step is to identify the audience and why you want to reach them. Perhaps you're looking for volunteers from that group? If so, write about the interesting items in the collection, possible uses of the materials, and opportunities for readers to actively participate by assisting researchers. Do you want to reach out to K–12 teachers? Through your newsletter's content, let them know how the local history reference collection can assist with teaching local and state history, social studies, U.S. history, and more. Before sending out such newsletters to school districts, check their protocols regarding such publications.

Creating the design of the newsletter will be the most time consuming as you decide on layout, fonts, and nameplate. Don't forget there are lots of free templates out there, including in basic word processing programs. But, once in place, you can base further issues on that template. For content, think repurpose! Press releases, blogs, annual reports, upcoming event lists (consider the time frame), information on volunteer projects, and more can be added judiciously to the newsletter. Allow enough time for the new content to be completed, as well as for possible review by library administrators and for revisions. To create a connection with readers, write articles in the first-person plural when possible. Articles about people, including staff, volunteers, researchers, and donors, can be of interest to your audience in addition to articles about items in the collection. Creating a story file of unpublished ideas and materials can help you if you need a quick backup story.

Will you have an online newsletter, hard copy, or both? Printing a hard copy requires more time and cost but can be helpful in getting it directly to the audience as well as having extra copies for distribution opportunities. An electronic copy can be posted on the library's website and is accessible from most computers. A print/electronic combination usually works best to reach multiple audiences. Think about other audiences that might be interested in the newsletter too—media outlets, previous donors of money, important people in the community (mayor, city council members), other libraries, and archives in your community. Speaking of repurposing: consider how many newsletter articles can become blog posts (and vice versa), encouraging patron feedback.

PUBLIC PRESENTATIONS

You will either love or hate the idea of giving public presentations. But they are one of the most powerful tools in your marketing tool kit. Connection to an audience can be made immediately, especially in the question-and-answer portion, and can gain you some valuable advocates. It can be helpful, and add to the comfort level, to create an adaptable template for public presentations consisting of basic information such as staff contacts, access to the collection (both on-site in the library and online), collection strengths, digital content, copying and scanning policies and fees, description of users, and more depending on your collection. But don't just use the template as the presentation. Adapting the presentation to the audience is key to engaging them. A unique, well-designed handout is helpful in taking your message beyond the presentation itself.

Presentations fall into two main categories—though they can also be combined. You can explore the collection, encouraging use and highlighting resources. Include a hands-on component so attendees can see what you have. Or you can prepare a presentation based on research in your collection, for example, "The Early Days in Our Town."

Who are some groups to consider for presentations? Interested groups that come immediately to mind are genealogists, historical societies, and local preservation groups. Lure genealogists to your collection by teaching them how to use databases like Ancestry.com and then show them all your other resources. Offer to speak at the regular meetings of the local historical society or preservation group (or better yet, host it at your institution). They may not have realized that the LHRC has older published local histories, newspapers, vertical files, and city directories—the raw materials they need to research local buildings and properties. Rotary clubs, the local PTA, school district in-service programs, and service clubs can be valuable audiences as well. So can other resident groups interested in the history of their houses, churches, schools, communities, and businesses. For example, in the Minnesota Twin Cities, there is a club of homeowners devoted to a fabulous collection of bungalows built in the early twentieth century. There might be such a group in your area. Checking in from time to time with a particular user group can provide real results. It's important that somebody oversees this. She doesn't have to be called a marketing specialist.

The Boston Public Library features a Local & Family History Lecture Series that shares information about the history of Boston and its neighborhoods along with tips and guides for those beginning genealogical research. The library recruits local experts to speak on topics of interest to the community. Check out their website at www.bpl.org/news/local_family_history_series.htm.

YOU'RE A MARKETING GURU!

Don't be intimidated by the prospect of marketing and outreach. Your library is probably doing a lot of the steps already—start by tapping into those and build from there as you learn about the audience for your local history reference collection. Have fun with marketing—some of the best marketing campaigns have probably looked goofy on paper but, once enacted, have gained attention due to their off-the-wall humorous slant. Be bold but not overwhelmed. And remember, there are a number of resources out there to help. A list of helpful guides is in the bibliography.

NOTES

1. Grace M. Malcolm, "Local History in Public Libraries," *Library Journal* 51, no. 3 (1926): 129.
2. Russell D. James and Peter J. Wosh, *Public Relations and Marketing for Archives* (Chicago: Society of American Archivists and New York: Neal-Schuman, 2011).
3. Ned Potter, "Marketing Your Library: An Interview with Terry Kendrick, Guru of Strategic Marketing in Libraries," *American Libraries* (November/December 2012), www.americanlibrariesmagazine.org/article/marketing-your-library.

CHAPTER 9

YOUR VIRTUAL LOCAL HISTORY REFERENCE COLLECTION

> "Tanisha, have you seen that really cool new mashup software that lets you put a historical walking tour of town onto a Google map? The library should be doing that—I think it's really easy!" Tanisha nods enthusiastically without committing herself and heads to her desk. Is it really easy? Can she find a tutorial to show her how it actually works? And, can she find a student or volunteer group to help her pull together the sites they want to highlight? She realizes that in just a few moments, she has gone from doubting she knows how to attempt such a project to assembling the workforce to get it done. Time to start writing up a proposal to see if her boss will be as enthusiastic as she is about work on what could be a demanding but high-visibility effort for her library.

IN THE CLOUD

Does it sometimes seem as though not only your head, but most of your library services are in the cloud(s)? That is today's reality. You work hard every day in a "brick and mortar" building, but know that many patrons you never see are accessing the library's catalog on the web, downloading e-books, using remote-access databases for homework, or instant messaging you with a question. There is no reason that the local history reference collection shouldn't also be an important feature of what we call the "digital branch." As we've mentioned earlier, the LHRC often has some of the most fascinating content in your library. Suggesting that it be used for library-wide online postings will keep your LHRC in the minds of both your patrons and colleagues.

In this chapter, we focus on the online presence of your LHRC specifically. We will cover the most common applications and techniques used by public libraries in showcasing their wonderful collections. And we'll also highlight some unusual ones and talk about some pitfalls.

DO I REALLY NEED TO DO THIS?

Yup, having an online presence is a given now, not optional. In the same way that online catalogs and e-mail or chat reference once seemed "above and beyond," informative and engaging websites and participation in social media are now basic avenues pursued by most public libraries. Let's start with the most basic method of virtually showcasing your collections and services: your page on your library's website.

It's rarely necessary to have your own separate website. Instead, get to know the webmaster for your library and find out if it's possible to have a separate local history page. Keeping track of the traffic in your LHRC, or related requests made of your reference staff, will help convince your webmaster that an LHRC-focused page will be a service to your patrons. Make sure the local history reference collection is easy to find from your home page. On many of the websites we viewed, local history is front and center, like at the Quincy (Illinois) Public Library (see figure 9.1). This tells us that these libraries receive enough questions about this material that they felt it was worth putting a link to the LHRC on their main navigation bar. That is capital in the currency of what patrons value. Trade on it where you can. A significant number of libraries also list their local history and genealogy collections under the broader heading of "Research." On other sites, local history or genealogy are virtually impossible to find. Don't dare your patrons to find you!

On a side note, a significant minority of LHCs we visited online have chosen a different route. Many have a blog that serves as their "front door." The drawback we see here is that a blog necessarily pushes older content below the first page. If the topics aren't indexed in some way (through subject tagging, for example), basic information may be out of sight. It's also important to have a constant section with your collection strengths, policies, and contact information that remains static for each viewing.

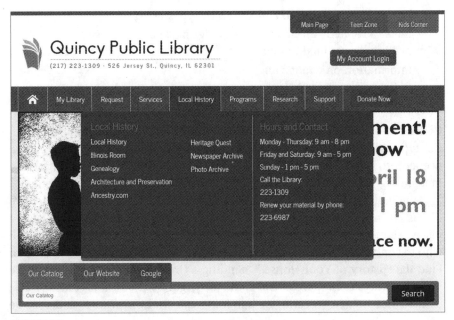

FIGURE 9.1

Local history on the library's navigation bar

Navigation bar, with Local History menu selected, from Quincy (Illinois)
Public Library website at http://quincylibrary.org

Other options are using your Facebook page as a main venue, a libguide
format, such as the Logan (Utah) Library,[1] or even a page on the Internet
Archive. One consideration is the age of your patrons: will older users find
you if your main access is on social media? There are no right or wrong methods; just make sure that library patrons see that you are an integral part of
the library's mission and services from your online presence.

WHAT BELONGS ON MY WEB PAGE?

Your page on your library's website will be the portal for all things local history and genealogy. We won't discuss website design here because for most
of us, the design of our page will follow the design template of our library's
website. Instead, we focus on the common features or virtual tools of most
library LHRC web pages. In brief they are:

- overviews of the collection: material types and examples;
- research or reference policies and contact information;

- how-to's and guides to collections or types of research;
- links to related resources, such as digitized content, forms, or library-provided databases;
- information on events; and
- links to other local history or genealogy resources, both local and regional/national.

Collection overviews can be as simple as a bulleted list of significant material types (city directories, county histories, vertical files, etc.). They can go deeper into how such sources can assist patrons in their search, and they can include digitized versions of parts or all of each type.

Being upfront about hours, policies, and special considerations, which we discussed in the chapter on access, is a service to your patrons. It's also a place to educate them about careful handling, before they arrive. Can they tell who to contact if they have further questions? How-to's and guides ("How to Find the History of Your House," "Finding a Grave in Our County," etc.) are proactive ways to prepare patrons, too (see figure 9.2). Mount guides you've created—or link to websites or handouts you find elsewhere, and receive

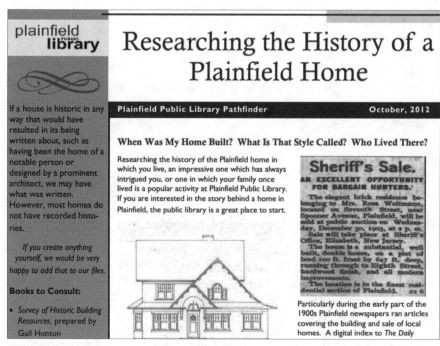

FIGURE 9.2

A how-to guide on a library website

permission to mount on your site. The house history research guide from the Plainfield (New Jersey) Public Library in the figure is easy to read on a web page and even asks for patrons to donate the products of their research to the library: www.plainfieldlibrary.info/pdf/Pathfinders/LH_Pathfinder%20 House%20Research.pdf.

We didn't find any libraries that followed the practice of some archives, which is to anticipate research topics and create guides to help locate materials in their holdings. But we think it is a practice that libraries could well emulate. If a tornado devastated your community, and you think that reporters, interested citizens, or History Day students will be coming to the library for information, why not create a guide that summarizes the event, and links patrons to any collections, publications, websites, or images you think they'll want to examine. It's proactive for frequently-asked-for topics. It can also allow you to promote items in your collection that are overlooked but that you think have rich potential.

"We have online collections mostly based on digital surrogates from our print collection, with a concentration on neighborhood history," wrote one librarian in response to our survey. These surrogates may become the patron-use versions of items too fragile to handle, except by occasional special appointment. Or they may simply be an additional way to promote use of the full collection—even an enticement to research. The most common types of digitized content found on LHC web pages are:

- cemetery surveys and listings;
- lists of local authors, elected officials, and so on;
- brief community histories;
- photograph and newspaper digitization databases, some massive and some merely representative or used as illustration;
- obituary or vital records indices, many with searchable interfaces;
- maps;
- local high school yearbooks, city directories, postcard collections, biographies of local notables and/or elected officials, and out-of-copyright local histories (some libraries have scanned just the indices to these books to promote their use); and
- lists, indices, and sometimes actual transcripts or recordings of oral history projects. One library, having chosen to participate in National Public Radio's "StoryCorps @ your library" program, mounted links to the interviews of local citizens.

And, of course, links to any history or genealogy databases provided by your library, including historical newspapers, census, and vital records sources.

Don't forget the rich websites provided by the Library of Congress's American Memory site and the National Archives.[2] Both of these sites, as well as websites from your state library and state archives, have special links for teachers, students, genealogists, military historians, and others. Finally, events, including classes and talks, are wonderful to advertise on this page, as long as you keep them up-to-date.

Many libraries have devised creative ways to showcase this deeper content (material that is several clicks into your website). A common method is the online exhibit. This can be a repurposed physical exhibit from your library, or one created just for online display (but we recommend repurposing wherever you can). There are an infinite number of ways to create such exhibits, from straightforward text with links to digitized content, to free and proprietary software to dress up your exhibit. We are fans of simple and straightforward, but you may have staff who want to experiment with newer methods. We also believe in the principle of trying new platforms and, essentially, playing with online toys. Within reason, this allows you to discover new options and can be a staff morale booster. Such projects are also perfect for interns, if your library sponsors such programs, as they are enhancements, but if they aren't completed to your satisfaction they won't hold up daily processes.

One version of an online exhibit is to re-create—or create from scratch—a scrapbook. There are a number of online scrapbooking programs. There is no reason why you couldn't mount images from your collections (and they don't all have to be photos!) as a showcase. Another idea is a brief video of scrapbook selections from the Plainfield (New Jersey) Public Library.[3] It captures the movement of flipping through a scrapbook without the need to find a "page flipping" software program.

Your local history reference collection can also serve as a very effective clearinghouse for lots of local history resources—and they don't all have to be from your own collection. Figure 9.3 shows an example from the Union County (North Carolina) Public Library site; it's quite straightforward with simple lists and links, bringing together a wealth of sources for further investigations, all in one place.[4]

This is simply a virtual version of your brochure rack with information on local historical organizations and events—but with much more depth. And if you link to other organizations, chances are they will link to you as well for some effective cross-promotion.

The Las Vegas-Clark County (Nevada) Library District also has a well-integrated approach to gathering together all the local and regional resources on Las Vegas history. The library staff didn't have to write or develop it; they just created an attractive, easy-to-use portal for all the timelines, histories,

FIGURE 9.3

Local history information clearinghouse on the LHC page

Union County Public Library, Monroe, North Carolina

databases, and special collection information they could find. They also made sure to link to this page from their Homework Help section.

MY LIBRARY USES SOCIAL MEDIA A LOT— SHOULD I USE IT, TOO?

Social media is, by now, nothing new. As we said earlier, it's become a basic part of most libraries' interaction with their patrons. Many of you reading this book have your own personal Facebook accounts, participate on Twitter, pin on Pinterest, post comments on news stories, vote online for competition television shows, and so on. And your libraries do the same. Depending on the size of your staff, you may be able to contribute to your library's postings yourself, or you may be required to submit content to someone else whose task this is. We don't have a recommendation about whether the LHRC should have its own Facebook page, blog, or Tumblr account. We just recommend that you be open to providing fun content—and informative postings on what your collection has to offer.

And don't forget, next to simply getting your message out there, the single biggest object of social media is to encourage interaction with your audience. That's why it's "social"! Ask questions of your patrons, post examples of their research, list new sources as they come in and ask who might want to use them. If they make comments or ask questions, make sure someone responds to them right away. It's not enough to be "liked" or even well liked. Reactions are the currency of social media.

Your library may have a carefully crafted plan for social media use. Or it may be in the experimental phase, trying different media to see what will work. If you are in a position to decide which application(s) will be used, we do advise you not to get overly invested in one particular service. They change, go out of business, or go out of fashion. The trick is to try new things and make your content work via various methods. Figure out a general approach and then make it work for each venue.

Here's what we mean: most libraries these days have some kind of presence on Facebook. Many of us have our own personal accounts and are familiar with "friending" each other and seeing whatever our friends post. Organizational or business accounts used to operate in just the same way. We would have campaigns to see how many "likes" our libraries could accumulate so we could reach all of our patrons. But, like all corporate ventures, Facebook doesn't exist to connect us to one another. It exists to make money for its shareholders. The free and unrestricted use of its service was essentially a "doorbuster" feature. We liked what we saw, and even counted on it to promote our services. So, the company feels confident that it can now require payment for what it used to offer for free. If you're not sure what this means, see figure 9.4. As you can see, coauthor Kathy's library's "likes" are more than 1,000. But the "reach" (the number of people who actually see the postings automatically in their newsfeed) could be as low as 357.[5] This is due to the changing algorithm, managed by Facebook itself, of how many people see the postings.

Week of 30 March–5 April

Albany County Public Library
Build Audience · Promote Page

See Insights

	LAST WEEK	PREVIOUS WEEK	TREND
Total Page Likes	1,152	1,150	0.2%
New Likes	2	0	0.0%
Weekly Total Reach	831	357	132.8%
People Engaged	55	20	175.0%

FIGURE 9.4

Your Facebook reach vs. likes

Courtesy of the Albany County Public Library, Laramie, Wyoming

Does this mean that every library should quit Facebook? Of course not! In this case it just means that we may have to consider use of Facebook as part of our PR budget. We pay for ads in our local newspapers or in other media, right? This is just another outlet and may in some cases be funds better spent than on older, less popular media. The point we are trying to make is that social media is a shifting landscape. It's important to be playing the game, because the patrons you want to reach are playing. But the rules change, and the stadiums can close without warning.

Kate Theimer, in her book *Web 2.0 Tools and Strategies for Archives and Local History Collections* explains it well:

> Sometimes the Medium is the Message: Web 2.0 doubters are sometimes skeptical of the motives of those who participate, saying that they're just doing it 'to be cool.' Archives and historical organizations rarely spend much time contemplating how to be cool, but they do think about how to be relevant. Using a [social media] tool doesn't guarantee relevance, but it does show that your organization is ready to try new things and interact with the public in new ways.

> Creating something like a blog, wiki, or podcast isn't something you
> should do just to be able to say your institution is doing something
> '2.0'; you should always have a mission-related goal for starting
> this kind of new project. At the same time, undertaking an outreach
> effort using a new technology does give the effort an added value
> . . . If you want to project an image of being forward thinking and
> people centered, then Web 2.0 tools may help to shape that image.[6]

Another consideration is what happens to the content you mount on social media. One cardinal rule: social media applications are not reliable long-term storage for your files! If you are using a service like an interactive timeline or an online scrapbook, you should be reading the fine print to make sure that what you mount via this company doesn't become their property in some way. Also, you may have spent a considerable amount of time researching and mounting the data. Make sure that you are saving it somewhere else so you can repurpose it. The last thing you want is for the service to go out of business and all your efforts to be lost. Twitpic is just the latest such venture to fold after encouraging thousands of users to mount their images on its platform. It made the news when it didn't inform them that the service—and their content—would become inaccessible in a very short time frame. Even venerable companies like Yahoo and Google choose to "sunset" older features of their browsers. They are more likely to give you advance notice, but your content is still without a home.

Again, the lesson is not to throw up your hands and decide not to play. It just means keeping up with the news about social media—and being ready to migrate to a new platform, if necessary.

We confess we were surprised at the narrow range of social media explored by most local history rooms represented in our survey. Some of the most common types of social media we have seen used by local history staff are discussed below.

Facebook

This application is especially useful for promotion of current exhibitions and events, collections, and connecting with other local organizations. The Onondaga County (New York) Public Library used its page to create a tie-in to a currently running documentary series: "If you're watching the PBS Roosevelt special you might want to stop by the library to see two photos of TR and his second wife Edith. Both pictures signed by them. They were part of a special 'contest' held in 1904 where the winner named their twins after Theodore and Edith." The currency of Facebook is even more critical than your web page. We were sorry to see several with the annotation (by Facebook—right at the top of the page . . .) "Page updated over a year ago."

Flickr

This is how many libraries showcase their visual materials without having to create their own portal. They just link to their library's Flickr page. It's not very elegant, but it does the job.

Blogs

WordPress and other blogging software are the main online outlet for a number of local history collections. Aside from the limitations we have noted, blogs too must be updated on a regular basis. Posting less than once a month is disappointing to the public. Be sure the library has the staff and interest to maintain this option.

A librarian at the Schaumburg Township (Illinois) District Library noted, "By far and away, though, the best thing I've done for our collection is to start the blog.[7] It puts our history out there, people find it easily and share their own comments on the postings and they get immersed in it and wind up subscribing to it. Best of all it gets my name and our library out there for visibility, donations and reference questions. Its success exceeded my wildest expectations. This year I hope to have 60,000 plus visits—up from 33,000 last year. It's continually growing."

Twitter, Tumblr, Instagram, and Pinterest

These are also popular, though they're still catching on. The latter two count heavily on visual content, so decide first if you have enough in your collection to "feed" this service. But, remember that old newspapers, city directories, maps, and even excerpts from books can be visually interesting. You don't *have* to mount photos! Chances are, participation in these venues will depend on having a staff member who is already exploring them and ready to work on an account for your collection. The Everett (Washington) Public Library is using Tumblr in much the way that most libraries use their Facebook page, showcasing their visual material and advertising library events (see figure 9.5).[8]

We also found quite a few imaginative examples of social media use—many we never would have imagined. Some are little known applications,

FIGURE 9.5

Using Tumblr for your content and to connect with patrons

Northwest Room, Everett Public Library, Everett, Washington

and others are "mashups": combining several applications or content from one source viewed in contrast or concert with another. Theimer notes, "The overwhelmingly predominant use of mashup technology among archives is to combine information about objects in the collections with geographic data."[9] We also found this to be true of local history collections. Some of our favorites are below.

SOCIAL MEDIA—HERE'S TO VARIETY!

The Albany (New York) Public Library's LHC has created Android/Apple apps for local history, allowing patrons to use their phones as a walking tour guide using maps and old photographs of the city.[10]

The Onandaga County Public Library is using its Instagram account to showcase visual content. Note that most of this very attractive content is not photographic, but historic print material (see figure 9.6).

There were fewer timelines than we would have predicted. If you decide to create or mount one for your community, it can be a great graphic or even a navigation tool for your page. A *Library Journal* issue contained a review of a handful of timeline software options. See Matt Enis's article "Time After Time, Product Spotlight" for an overview of several current

FIGURE 9.6

Instagram can show the visual appeal of printed materials too

Used with permission of the Onondaga County Public Library.

timeline applications.[11] The Oak Lawn (Illinois) Public Library is using an app called Capzles.[12] Like many apps, it takes your content and plugs it into a program providing easy navigation for your patrons.[13]

The city of Orange, California, has a fun section called "History's Mysteries" with unidentified photos.[14] While not technically a social media application, it is certainly encouraging patron interaction and engagement with its resources and staff.

Another library has used Google Maps to show local historic homes. Maps, whether historic items from your collection or current maps with other information superimposed on them, are great online tools—a perfect example of a mashup. Several other libraries created map and photograph mashups to show local historic site locations. The library in Franklin Park, Illinois, used Google Maps, while the Kalamazoo (Michigan) Public Library created an interactive map using a lesser-known app called Tagwhat.[15]

You can also use apps like Historypin to integrate images with interactive local maps. The Oak Lawn Public Library used Google Maps and U.S. Geological Survey maps to show different facets of its community history. And it has used photos in its Flickr account to create a "Then and Now" exhibit of local views, all in Historypin (see figure 9.7).

FIGURE 9.7

Historypin uses maps and visuals

Image courtesy of the Oak Lawn Public Library, shared on Historypin.org

We were surprised that more libraries are not using wikis, a service that allows a group of users to contribute and edit content. The state of Wyoming maintains The "Wyoming Authors Wiki" to which librarians across the state add biographical and bibliographical information.[16] The New Bern-Craven County (North Carolina) Public Library's Kellenberger Room page links to this wiki, which they use to pull together a number of digitized print materials, indices, and oral histories. It's a very flexible format but not as attractive or flashy as other, newer methods. See http://kellenbergerroom.pbworks.com.

The Kalamazoo Public Library has a resource page on local cemeteries that uses images from Sanborn Fire Insurance maps combined with current maps from Google to pinpoint cemetery locations, as well as notes about the availability of gravestone transcriptions. They have mounted videos from a variety of local history presentations as well as a clip from the original Glenn Miller film recording of "I've Got a Gal in Kalamazoo." These could also have been mounted on a free YouTube channel and linked to their website. So many options!

EVERY DAY THERE'S SOMETHING NEW! HOW DO I LEARN HOW TO USE THEM?

Not familiar with the latest applications? Take a little time to explore "23 Things for Librarians." The Public Library of Charlotte Mecklenburg County (North Carolina) has been a leader in developing the original "23 Things . . ." website. They assembled 23 examples of what was known as "Web 2.0" when it first began.[17] Each "thing" is explained, links are given to tutorials, practice exercises are provided, and in some cases assistance is provided via web chat—and it's all free. It is entirely self-paced, but some groups have found that doing the series together gives them group support and the advantages of mutual problem solving. Online interactivity, even if not live, does provide a backlog of user questions and answers. It's a really easy way to dip your toes in, try out a number of new applications, and see what might work for you.

Since this project began, it has inspired many offshoots and similar projects: "23 Mobile Things," "23 Things On a Stick" (from Minnesota, a nod to the food choices at their state fair), "23 Things for Archivists," and so on. Your state may have run its own version (in Wyoming, it was called "Get on the Bus"), but most can be found by simply searching the Internet for "23 Things."

YouTube and Vimeo are also great sources for tutorials. There is almost no process, software, or research query that *someone* hasn't narrated as an online video. They vary in quality but are absolutely worth exploring. We also recommend asking younger staff members what social media they use most. Individual tastes will, of course, vary. But you may discover that you have in-house expertise you've been overlooking.

I THINK I SHOULD BE DIGITIZING MY COLLECTIONS: WHAT DO I DO?

When we surveyed public librarians, we asked: "What could we help you with? Name one or two things you would like to learn from our forthcoming book." We heard back loud and clear that digitization—when, why, and mostly how—was a major concern. Since neither of us is an expert at digitizing materials, nor creating collections or databases of digitized files, we will not pretend to provide a manual on this topic. What we can do, instead, is give you a solid list of references on this process and some useful questions to ask yourself before you dive in.

We also should start by encouraging you to begin by talking with the library's IT staff, or whoever at your library manages your technology and online presence. Before planning begins on scanning and mounting digital files, you should ask about any limitations or specifications related to your website, server space, and existing equipment. As you explore this process, you should consider the IT staff as in-house experts. Chances are you won't get far with the project if you haven't begun by discussing it with them first.

Now, we know that our recommendations concerning social media may seem to boil down to "everyone's doing it, so you should too." That would be a fair comment, and we're actually OK with that idea. Everyone is doing it, and if you want to reach your patrons, you should be ready to meet them where they are. Also, most versions are free. The cost is mostly staff time, which you of course need to weigh carefully.

However, we are not convinced that "everyone" is using our digitized content. And the time and equipment are not free. We do feel that this is a marvelous way to give patrons easy access to sometimes fragile or inaccessible materials. We simply recommend that careful attention be paid to which materials warrant digitization. The focus ought to be on the following types of materials:

- in constant demand or in danger of overuse;
- fragile, oversized, or awkward to use;
- relating to popular topics;
- relating to topics or materials you particularly wish to promote; and
- not covered by copyright (see appendix F for a guide to determine what material is copyright-free).

As you consider digitizing items from the LHRC, do keep in mind that "visually interesting material" does not mean just photographs. City directories, images (including text, ads, etc.) from microfilm of newspapers or Sanborn maps, pages from old books, telephone books, flyers, maps, and so on can all be fascinating if captured attractively. Or you could use images from a local historical society or archives and make it a great collaboration.

SHOULD I GO IT ALONE, OR PARTICIPATE IN A LARGER PROJECT?

If you are satisfied that there is a reason to digitize an item or collection, your next consideration is whether to digitize the materials in-house or contribute them (loan the originals) to a larger digital collection. Refer to our collaboration chapter for a couple of examples of "homegrown" digital collaboration projects. Many public libraries have already joined statewide, regional, or national digitization projects—either by loaning their materials to the larger organizations for digitization or by depositing digital images into a larger database. Some have chosen, instead, to link their smaller sets of files to these major databases. The disadvantage of the latter option is that your material might not be integrated into the larger project's search engine and thus be less discoverable. It would be worth contacting your state library to determine if it has such a project ongoing and what its interest may be in including your collections.

Another option is to collaborate with Internet Archive, which has been building a vast library of scanned out-of-copyright print material. A good example is from the Waltham (Massachusetts) Public Library. They provide links to local history publications, scanned for them and hosted on Internet Archive's site. If this is an option you'd like to pursue, visit their scanning page and contact them about your materials. They also invite your library ("partner organizations") to upload previously scanned materials to Internet Archive. Note that you might want to consult them about file and metadata (descriptive) requirements, if you haven't already done the scanning.

And, of course, the Digital Public Library of America is working to aggregate many of these state and regional digital repositories into one searchable interface. They are starting with just a select group of collaborative projects but seem intent on creating one portal for accessing a multitude of images and files.

If your library is small, or your audience is likely to remain entirely local, you may prefer to conduct your own digitization project and make the main portal your web page. We still strongly recommend some kind of record in the online catalog to alert patrons to the existence of these new, digitized versions of your collections. It may be a separate catalog record or a link to the digitized version in the record for the print item.

An excellent overview of the digitization process for small libraries is found in Nicci Westbrook's chapter, "Digital Collections" in *Technology for Small and One-Person Libraries: A LITA Guide.*[18] In one short chapter, she covers:

- financial resources and administrative support needed;
- criteria for selecting the material;
- potential partnerships for collections;
- copyright considerations and resources;
- choosing a content delivery platform—and its long-term stability;
- metadata guidelines;
- choosing equipment and software;
- preserving digitized files; and
- assessing collection use.

We even found a nifty "Library Digitization Cost Calculator" from the Digital Library Federation that can help gauge how much it might cost to mount such a project. It's online at http://statelibrarync.org/plstats/digitization_calculator.php.

WHAT ABOUT NEWSPAPERS?

We discussed the digitization of newspapers in our chapter on access. The first question to ask is whether scanned or microfilmed versions of local newspapers already exist. If they do, there is no sense in pursuing the costly option of digitizing these items.

Before you begin such a project—or seek funding to do it—please consult your state archives and state library. Many states have already undertaken massive newspaper microfilming and digitization projects of which you may be unaware. An excellent place to start is this list of historical newspapers online, http://viewshare.org/views/refhelp. If the state library or archives is digitizing other newspapers in your state, you can certainly alert them to any titles you have in your collection that they have missed. Google News is another venue chosen by at least one library for digitizing its older newspapers. And Internet Archive is another potential partner or host for this project.

JUMP IN—THE WATER'S WARM

Regardless of whether you choose to keep it very simple or experiment with new apps and mount major projects, we encourage you to try new ideas and keep patrons coming back to your page for more. In addition to the examples above, we thought we'd leave you with an example from the Austin (Texas) History Center. It's really just a traditional FAQ page with questions about Austin history (see figure 9.8). But it's been cast as a quiz to challenge local history buffs. There are opportunities here for contests, prizes, and other kinds of engagement with your audience.

We hope you will play with new applications, keep web pages fresh and updated—and most of all have fun exploring all the new "toys" and ways to promote local history on the Internet.

NOTES

1. Logan History, Logan Library, Logan, Utah, http://library.loganutah.org/Archives.

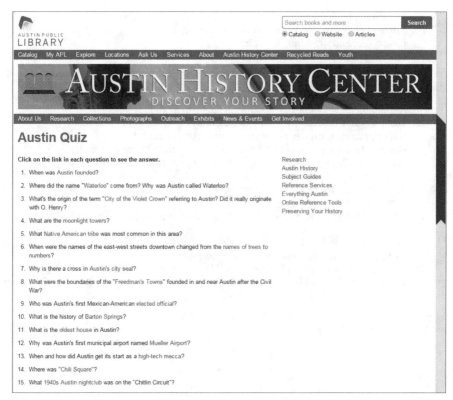

FIGURE 9.8

Turn an FAQ into a fun quiz

Courtesy of the Austin History Center, Austin Public Library,
http://library.austintexas.gov/ahc/austin-quiz

2. American Memory, Library of Congress, Washington, D.C., www.memory.loc
   .gov and Research Our Records, National Archives, Washington, D.C., www
   .archives.gov/research.
3. Historical Plainfield Scrapbooks, Plainfield Public Library, Plainfield, New
   Jersey, www.plainfieldlibrary.info/Departments/LH/LH_scrapbooks.html.
4. Seek Local History, Union County Public Library, Monroe, North Carolina,
   www.union.lib.nc.us/genealogy_local_history.asp.
5. Facebook web page update, e-mail to Kathy Marquis, September 10, 2014.
6. Kate Theimer, *Web 2.0 Tools and Strategies for Archives and Local History
   Collections* (New York: Neal-Schuman, 2010), 207.
7. Tony Kierna, *Tony's Genealogy Blog* at the Schaumburg Township (Illinois)
   District Library, http://genealogywithtony.wordpress.com/.
8. Tumblr for Northwest History Room Archives, Northwest History Room, Everett
   Public Library, Everett, Washington, http://nwhistoryroomarchives.tumblr
   .com/.

9. Theimer, *Web 2.0 Tools and Strategies,* 180.

10. Albany: Then and Now, Troy Web Consulting, Troy, New York, http://historythenandnow.com/about.html.

11. Matt Enis, "Time After Time: Product Spotlight," *Library Journal* 139, no. 14 (2014): 34, http://lj.libraryjournal.com/2014/09/digital-content/time-after-time-product-spotlight/#.

12. Capzles Social Storytelling, Oak Lawn Public Library, Oak Lawn, Illinois, www.capzles.com/#/33c0b0c7-a50d-4b27-aa46-e1a725da5094/.

13. For a simpler timeline, see the Boone County (Kentucky) Public Library's timeline navigation bar at www.bcpl.org/cbc/doku.php.

14. Historic Orange Preservation Online, Orange Public Library Local History Collection, Orange Public Library, Orange, California, www.cityoforange.org/localhistory/default.htm.

15. Tagwhat Interactive Map, Kalamazoo Public Library, Kalamazoo, Michigan, www.kpl.gov/local-history/tagwhat/.

16. The Wyoming Authors Wiki, WyomingAuthors.org, http://wiki.wyomingauthors.org/.

17. Learning 2.0, Public Library of Charlotte and Mecklenburg County, Charlotte, North Carolina, http://plcmc12-about.blogspot.com.

18. Nicci Westbrook, "Digital Collections," in *Technology for Small and One-Person Libraries: A LITA Guide,* by Rene J. Erlandson and Rachel A. Erb (New York: American Library Association, 2013).

APPENDIX A | LOCAL HISTORY COLLECTION SURVEY INSTRUMENT

1. Does your library have a separate local history or genealogy section (apart from materials in the open shelves)?

   ☐ Yes   ☐ No

2. What is the primary focus of your local history collection?

   ☐ Local history

   ☐ Genealogy

   ☐ Both

   ☐ Other (please specify)_____

3. What types of materials are included in your collection? (check all that apply)

   ☐ Published materials (books, magazines, city directories, pamphlets, etc.)

   ☐ Newspapers on microfilm

   ☐ Ephemera (vertical file, hanging files, clippings, etc.)

   ☐ Photographs

   ☐ Unpublished materials (letters, diaries, and scrapbooks)

   ☐ Oral history interviews

   ☐ Other (please specify)_____

4. Do you require patrons to register to use your local history collection?

   ☐ Yes   ☐ No

5. Do you have a dedicated staff position, or a portion of a position, for this collection?

   ☐ Yes, under 10 hours per week

   ☐ Yes, 10 to 20 hours per week

   ☐ Yes, 20+ hours per week

   ☐ No, library staff assists patrons with this collection as part of their regular reference duties

6. Is your local history collection closed when it is not staffed?

   ☐ No, it's open whenever the library is open

   ☐ Yes, it must be staffed to be open

7. Are materials in your local history collection included in the library's catalog?

   ☐ Yes, using the library's main cataloging conventions (Dewey, LC, etc.)

   ☐ Yes, using a special cataloging system

   ☐ No, there is a finding system with the collection

   ☐ No, it is just a browsing collection with no finding system

8. If you answered the previous question with "Yes, using a special cataloging system" or "No, there is a finding system with the collection," how would you describe that system?

   _____

9. Is your local history collection covered by a collection policy?

   ☐ Yes, by a policy specific to the local history collection

   ☐ Yes, by the library's overall collection policy, but not one specific to this collection

   ☐ No, there is not a collection policy for this collection

10. If you answered "Yes, by a policy specific to our local history collection," please paste a link to the policy if it is available online, or include your e-mail if we may request it.

    _____

11. How do you promote your collection? (check all that apply)

    ☐ Materials in the main library catalog

    ☐ Collection has a page on the main library website

    ☐ Signs outside of collection in library

    ☐ Brochures in library

    ☐ Brochures elsewhere in community

    ☐ Talks given to groups interested in local history

    ☐ Work with local schools for National History Day

    ☐ Other (please specify)_____

    _____

12. Who are the users of your local history materials? (check all that apply)

    ☐ Genealogists

    ☐ Historians

    ☐ Authors

    ☐ Teachers

    ☐ K–12 students

    ☐ College/university students

    ☐ Professionals (journalists, engineers, lawyers, etc.)

    ☐ Others (please specify)_____

    _____

13. Is there anything else you'd like to tell us about your collection—its name, web address, strengths, or what makes it special?

    _____

14. Tell us about your library. (optional)

    Library Name: _____

    City/Town: _____

    State:_____

15. Final question! What could we help you with? Name one or two things you would like to learn from our forthcoming book, *Local History Reference Collections for Public Libraries*:

    _____

Thank you very much for your help!

RUSA GUIDELINES FOR ESTABLISHING LOCAL HISTORY COLLECTIONS

Developed by the Local History Committee of the History Section, Reference and Adult Services Association (RUSA), American Library Association, June 1979. Reaffirmed by the Reference and Adult Services Division Board of Directors, January 1993. Revised 2005, and approved January 2006 by the Reference and User Services Association Board of Directors. [Revised, approved by History Section Executive Committee, and sent to RUSA Standards and Guidelines Committee (March 2012).] Revised and approved by RUSA Board, May 2012. These guidelines can be accessed online at www.ala.org/rusa/resources/guidelines/guidelinesestablishing.

Introduction

These guidelines are intended to assist librarians in establishing local history collections. In surveying the literature about the collecting of local materials it is apparent that many have already written about the use and the maintenance of the various media employed in local history.

Guidelines

1.0 Considerations before making a commitment to developing a local history collection
    1.1 Research and understand the history that is unique to the locality.
    1.2 Establish and maintain a dialog between local institutions (museums, academic libraries, local archives), societies (both genealogical and historical), and agencies (county, city, and state). Consider what is currently being collected, what services are needed, to what depth such collections are being developed,

and what collaborative or cooperative agreements are needed. Determine the most suitable repository for particular materials with respect to use, dissemination, and preservation.

2.0 Scope and Services of the Collection

2.1 Identify the focus and depth of the collection. Limiting factors may include geography, format, and space within the repository.

2.2 Identify the range of services that will be provided, onsite and remotely.

3.0 Collection Development

3.1 Write an acquisitions policy for collecting local history materials.

3.2 State the intended geographic collection area.

3.3 Describe those materials desired by the institution and the extent to which they will be collected.

3.4 Describe the formats to be collected.

3.5 Identify the types of materials that will not be collected by the institution. Other institutions may be better equipped to handle a given type of material. Some items may not be accepted due to preservation issues.

3.6 Identify those subject areas which will be acquired only on a cooperative basis.

3.7 Write a policy on acceptance of materials through gifts and bequests. Include forms for "deeds of gift." See the Society of American Archivists web page for detailed guidelines.

3.8 Write a policy on de-accessioning that is in keeping with the overall policy of the institution. Bear in mind policies already established by other professional organizations. [See http://www2.archivists.org/sites/all/files/GuidelinesFor ReappraisalAndDeaccessioningDRAFT.pdf for de-accessioning guidelines.]

4.0 Collection Location and Access

4.1 Establish the local history collection in an identifiable place in the library, separate from other collections.

    1. Create a separate area on the library's web page for the local history collection.

    2. Digitize fragile items for access on the local history webpage.

4.2 Provide an environment that is conducive to the preservation of materials.

4.3 Designate a secure space for the local history collection with proper provisions for monitoring materials.

4.4 Provide a clear and visible access policy.

4.5 Provide equipment and workspace sufficient to use the collection.

4.6 Utilize professional staff to collect, process, maintain and provide access to the local history collection. Professionals may be assisted by trained paraprofessionals and volunteers.

4.7 Understand copyright implications that may affect access.

5.0 Fiscal Considerations

5.1 Provide a budget for staffing the collection.

5.2 Provide a budget sufficient to acquire, process, and preserve the local history collection.

5.3 Provide a budget for physical and bibliographic access to the collection.

5.4 Provide a budget for reproduction, reformatting, and/or digitization of rare and fragile materials.

5.5 Provide a budget for public relations.

5.6 Develop a policy for a reproduction fee schedule.

Bibliography for RUSA Guidelines

Balloffet, Nelly, and Jenny Hille. *Preservation and Conservation for Libraries and Archives.* Chicago: American Library Association, 2005.

Carvalho, Joseph. "Organizing a Local History Collection in a Small Public Library." *Library Quarterly* 8, no. 1–2 (1987–88): 109–18.

Cox, Richard. *Documenting Localities: A Practical Model for American Archivists and Manuscript Curators.* Lanham, Md.: Scarecrow, 1996.

Finch, Elsie Freeman. *Advocating Archives: An Introduction to Public Relations for Archivists.* Lanham, Md.: Society of American Archivists and Scarecrow Press, 2003.

Hackbart-Dean, Pam, and Elizabeth Slomba. *Processing Decisions for Manuscripts and Archives.* Washington, DC: Association of Research Libraries, 2009.

Harden, Johanna Jaeggli. "Saving the Past for the Future! Part 1: Deciding What to Save for a Local History Collection." *Colorado Libraries* 27, no. 4 (Winter 2001): 43–44.

Harden, Johanna Jaeggli. "Saving the Past for the Future! Deciding What to Save, Part 2: Preserving What Is Saved." *Colorado Libraries* 29, no. 3 (Fall 2003): 44–46.

Kurtz, Michael J. *Managing Archival and Manuscript Repositories.* Chicago: Society of American Archivists, 2004.

Kyving, David E., and Myron A. Marty. *Nearby History: Exploring the Past Around You.* Lanham, Md.: Rowman & Littlefield Publishers, 2010.

Marquis, Kathy, and Leslie C. Waggener. "Historical Collections: Is Adding One Right for Your Public Library?" *Public Libraries* 50, no. 2 (March 2011): 42–48.

North Carolina Library Association. "Establishing and Maintaining a Local History Collection." *North Carolina Libraries* 46 (Summer 1988): 70–84.

Ogden, Sherelyn, ed. *Preservation of Library & Archival Materials: A Manual.* Andover, Mass.: Northeast Document Conservation Center, 1999.

Phillips, Faye. *Local History Collections in Libraries.* Englewood, CO: Libraries Unlimited, 1995.

RUSA grants permission to use their "Guidelines for Establishing Local History Collections" in the book: *Local History Reference Collections for Public Libraries.*

American Association for State and Local History book series, various titles (www.aaslh.org/reports.htm).

| # COLLECTION DEVELOPMENT POLICY TEMPLATE

The Ticleton Local History Collection Development Policy, Twilfitt Public Library

1. *Mission Statement*

   See chapter 3 of this book for guidelines on writing a mission statement.

   For example:

   The Ticleton Local History Collection promotes the understanding and exploration of Ticleton history, culture, and architecture. Our local history collection educates community members by collecting, preserving, and providing access to published materials about Ticleton, and by providing educational programming related to those materials. The Ticleton Local History Collection does not attempt to provide research materials available through other special collections in [your state]; however the value of this collection lies in its depth, breadth, and scope of comprehensive survey of Ticleton.

2. *Responsibility for the Collections*
   - Who is vested with the responsibility for determining the policies in this document? Don't think in terms of the names of those people, but what are their positions in your library?
   - Who is vested in carrying out the policy?
   - Who can make changes to the policy as the needs of the library change?

For example:

Final authority for the determination of the policies in this document is vested in the Twilfitt Public Library Board of Trustees. It has delegated the responsibility for implementing this policy to the Library Director, who, in turn, delegates to the Local History Librarian the responsibility for selection of materials in the special areas of this department. The recommendations of the Local History Librarian are always subject to review by the Director. It is the responsibility of the Local History Librarian, the Library Director, and the Board to see that this policy is updated should new collecting areas be added or should priorities for the collection be revised.

It is the function of librarians to select and to withdraw library materials, and to advise on their use. They are qualified through training and expertise; however, they must of necessity work within the limitations of space and budget. Recognizing that sensitivity to the needs and interests of the community is essential to the development of library collections, the Ticleton Local History Collection welcomes advice and suggestions from patrons, trustees, and authorities in various fields. Librarians, however, are responsible for judging the needs of their collection and their community, and they must make the final choices. The Director and the Local History Librarian will determine appropriate gifted items to the local history collection. The Director and the Board will determine if a purchase to the local history collection is warranted (see item 6 below for more information).

3. **Purpose of the Collection**

   - Who is the clientele for the local history collection, either existing or those you want to attract?
   - What types of programs will be supported by the collection—research, exhibits, community outreach, publications, more?

4. **Nature of the Collection**

   A short narrative statement summarizing the characteristics of the collection and its use.

   For example:

   The Ticleton Local History Collection is located in the Theodore Ticleton Room at the Twilfitt Public Library and houses a browsable collection of primary and secondary sources consisting of books, periodicals, maps, pamphlets, serials, directories, electronic databases, and other materials about the civic, social, religious, cultural, political, and economic life of Ticleton past and present. The materials are accessible to the public, but do not circulate. Duplicate copies of local history items may be available in the circulating collections. Rare and unique materials as well as small items are not browsable, but are accessible at the library's circulation desk. Patrons may duplicate materials with digital camera, scanner, or library photocopiers with permission from library staff.

5. *Primary Areas of Collecting*

- For what geographic area are you planning to collect and for what time periods?
- Will you collect everything about the community or a representative sample, or are you trying to fill a niche, such as only seeking genealogical materials or the history of businesses in the area?
- What will not be collected in terms of subject and format?
- What are the collection's present strengths and weaknesses? How will you deal with the weaknesses?
- Will you take materials in languages other than English (consider the ethnic population in your area)? What staff members can make changes to the policy as the needs of the library change?

For example:

An active effort is made to add to the recognized strengths of the collections in the Ticleton Local History Collection. The Local History Librarian solicits gifts, searches the library's reference and circulating collections for transfers, consults with dealers, and examines publishers' catalogs and reviews media for the purchase or acquisition of the following types of material:

- Published and near-print materials that record the history, development, and the current state of affairs of Ticleton.
- Published and near-print materials that record the history and ancestry of Ticleton families.
- Published and near-print materials that record the cultural heritage of past and present ethnic and religious groups in the community.
- Published and near-print materials that contribute to a better understanding of the area's geography, demographics, and architecture.

- Published and near-print materials written by or attributed to local authors, fictional works set in Ticleton, and some critical and biographical works of the area's major literary figures.
- Published and near-print materials that provide instruction relating to genealogy, local history, preservation, and similar topics.

Acceptance of additions to the permanent collections shall be made on the following conditions:

- Consistency with the library's mission and the purpose of the local history collection;
- Authority, authenticity, and reliability;
- Educational, interpretive, and/or exhibit value;
- Adequacy of documentation;
- Intrinsic value possessing relative beauty, rarity, uniqueness, association with important events or individuals, age and acceptable condition;
- Clear title available from the source of acquisition;
- Ability of the library to care properly for and use the acquisition;
- Price.

In selecting materials for purchase or accepting donations, the library shall be cognizant of the space limitations inherent in the local history collection, the potential usefulness of the item, and the suitability of the material in the Ticleton Local History Collection as opposed to other area collections. The Library, in accepting donated materials for placement in the local history collection, does so with the understanding that the donated materials will be a long-term asset to the local history collection.

6. *Limitations on the Addition of Materials*

- How will gifts to the library's local history collection be handled, and by whom?
- How will your library handle unwanted gifts?
- What about damaged items? Will your library accept them as gifts?
- How will physical and intellectual transfer of ownership to your library occur for donated materials?
- What if a donor asks your library to appraise the item she wishes to donate?
- What if a donor wants to place a restriction on the donated item?

For example:

Gifts to the Twilfitt Public Library are evaluated under the same conditions as purchased materials. The Library Director and the Board of Trustees may decline to accept for the Ticleton Local History Collection any gift of material that seems inappropriate to the collection or that would be more appropriate in another repository. In such cases, the would-be donor should be informed of the scope of the Ticleton Local History Collection and, if possible, put in touch with an institution that might wish to accept the offered gift.

The Twilfitt Public Library's justifications for not accepting gifts may include, but not necessarily be limited to the following:

- Outside the library's scope;
- Deteriorated or lacking in physical integrity;
- Cannot be preserved by the Twilfitt Public Library;
- Inauthentic;
- Duplicate;
- Irrelevant;
- Of doubtful future use to the library.

Condition often forms an important criterion in determining whether to accept a gift for the Ticleton Local History Collection. If material is in such poor condition that its shelving and use would be difficult, and if the cost of restoration by a qualified restorer is beyond the Library's budget, the potential donor should be encouraged to include as part of the gift the sum necessary to restore it to usable condition.

As already noted, the limited shelving space in the Ticleton Local History Collection is a consideration in adding volumes to the collection. The Library Director and Trustees may find it necessary to decline a large gift of material of a kind actively included in the collection should there be insufficient shelving or space to accommodate it. If the decision is made to accept a gift that cannot be housed in the Ticleton Local History Collection under existing conditions, funding to purchase shelving could either be solicited from the donor of the materials or appropriated from the discretionary funds of the Library Trustees. The long-term storage of unique local history or genealogical material outside of the Ticleton Local History Collection is to be avoided. Similarly, the lack of staffing to accession a sizeable addition to the local history collection may also determine whether a gift is accepted. If it is desirable to accept a substantial gift that cannot be promptly cataloged by library personnel, or if there is no staff member who can prepare adequate cataloging, the wherewithal to hire a qualified cataloger should be sought from the donor or taken from other library funds.

Donors should be informed that library staff cannot be expected to provide an appraisal of donated material. The usual procedure is for the donor to pay for any appraisal desired.

Donors of material to the Ticleton Local History Collection will be routinely asked to provide written documentation acknowledging the gift to the library and giving the Board of Trustees the right to dispose of the gift as they see fit.

Major gifts with restrictions attached may be accepted, but the provisions of the gift must be stated in writing by the donor, and signed by the donor, the Library Director, and the Chair of the Board of Trustees. The Twilfitt Public Library will ask that these restrictions have a limited time frame. The Library may remove these restrictions only after the time restriction has passed or by taking the appropriate legal steps recommended by the City Solicitor or other legal counsel.

7. *Weeding the Collection*

- What are the criteria for weeding your local history collection?
- Will you dispose of originals when an item(s) is reformatted?
- How often will you review the collection for weeding?

For example:

In keeping with the purpose, nature, and scope of the Ticleton Local History Collection of the Twilfitt Public Library as defined in this document, weeding of the collection does not follow the same guidelines as those set out for the Circulating and General Reference collections. The collections housed in the local history collection are part of the heritage of Ticleton and, as such, have more permanent historic and cultural value.

However, considerations of physical space limitations, combined with the need to add new materials to the collections, make it imperative that the composition of the collection be reevaluated periodically. Simultaneously, the changing nature of technology, advances in preservation practices, and availability of previously scarce materials in reprint, digital, or micro format are changing the range of options available to special collections librarians in managing their collections.

7.1 Weeding Criteria

The first consideration in applying a weeding policy to these collections is the recognition of three distinct categories of materials and the nature of each category.

These categories can be defined as follows:

7.1.a. Permanent Intrinsic Value: Items and collections that have permanent intrinsic value, including such individual items as:

- First editions of local histories, biographies and fictional works by local authors;
- Items signed by, or from the collections of, prominent local residents;
- Original documents, pamphlets, and maps;
- Other materials deemed to be of a similar nature.

All items of permanent intrinsic value are valuable to the cultural heritage of Ticleton in and of themselves. These materials should be preserved and permanently retained.

7.1.b. Permanent Informational Value: Other materials in the collections are of permanent value for their informational content, but are not intrinsically valuable. Items that fall into this category are candidates for replacement and/or reformatting should the condition of the material or space considerations make it desirable to do so. Informational value can be preserved by replacing items in poor condition with reprints or micro formats. Space-consuming series can be replaced with digital or micro formats as they become available, although digital versions of materials with permanent informational value should not be the only medium retained.

7.1.c. Temporary Informational Value: Time-sensitive materials, current informational reference sources, how-to books of a technological nature, and some periodicals have a finite period of usefulness. Items that fall into this category should be routinely evaluated and removed or replaced as appropriate.

7.2 Frequency of Weeding

As with the other collections of the library, weeding should not be a major project undertaken every several years or when there is no longer room to shelve the materials. The collection as a whole should be reviewed periodically, keeping in mind the purpose, nature and scope of the collections as outlined in the sections above. Based on the weeding criteria described in section 7.1, some areas of the collection will require more frequent review than others depending upon the category into which they fall.

7.2.a. Permanent Intrinsic Value: Little or no weeding of materials that fall into this category is to be expected.

7.2.b. Permanent Informational Value: Management of materials in this category is an ongoing process within the department, driven primarily by condition of the material, availability of replacements (in some format), and space availability.

7.2.c. Temporary Informational Value: Systematic review of materials in this category should be conducted on an ongoing and rotating basis, with all areas of the collection receiving attention every two years.

7.3 Disposal

Most materials withdrawn from the Ticleton Local History Collection are sold through periodic book sales of the Friends of the Twilfitt Public Library. Proceeds of these sales are used by the library for funding the cost of rebinding other materials or for other purchases. If rare, valuable items are for some reason withdrawn, they are sold with the assistance of a rare book dealer.

■ ■ ■

Much of the text for this policy was taken from the collection development policy for the Berkshire Athenaeum at the Pittsfield (MA) Public Library. Our thanks to Kathleen Reilly for allowing us to use and modify their policy for our publication.

APPENDIX D | **CONDITION OF ITEM(S) FORM**

_____   _____

NAME OF PERSON REPORTING DAMAGE   DATE

Item Identification

_____   _____

TITLE OF ITEM(S)   LOCATION

_____

DESCRIPTION OF ITEM(S)

Problem Identification

☐ Pages torn, binding broken, cover damaged
☐ Mold damage
☐ Item(s) dirty, bent, brittle, fragile, torn, folded, stained, foxing
☐ Insect or rodent damage
☐ Yellowed sticky tape
☐ Materials disarranged
☐ Item(s) container damaged or brittle
☐ Overloaded folders or boxes
☐ Label(s) missing
☐ Graffiti
☐ Suggested additional subject or name entry

☐ Suggested changes to catalog record
☐ Item(s) endangered by current storage condition
☐ Other (please specify) _____

Comments/Explanation of the Problem

Forwarded to _____

Problem resolved by:

_____   _____
                    NAME   DATE

| # ALBANY COUNTY PUBLIC LIBRARY GENEALOGY TRAINING WORKSHEET

Let's start with what we have in the library's Wyoming Room.

Find the basic Laramie, Wyoming history, *Laramie, Gem City*. Look up a name in the back and find it in the book (index citations like T-33 mean section T, page 33)

Name: _____

Something interesting about the person: _____

_____

Look at the call number of *Laramie, Gem City*. This is where most of the published Laramie information is on the shelf—just a few other reminiscences and local histories. Do you see the picture book, *Laramie,* from Arcadia Pubs.? A great book to show patrons! Most of the photos came from the Laramie Plains Museum in town—a great place to refer patrons.

Now, find this person, or someone with the same last name in a *city directory*.

Where did they live? _____

Did they own the home? _____

What was their occupation? _____

If the city directory has a "cross directory" (street-by-street listing) at the back, what was a neighbor's name and occupation? _____

_____

Find the bio file near the end of the *Wyoming Pamphlet File,* which would contain a clipping about this person, if we found one. Did we? _____

_____

Extra credit: can you find their home on the *Sanborn Maps* (in our online databases)?

Let's try the *obituary indices.* Is the person in the *printed index volumes* in the Wyoming Room?

Try the *online version of the obituary index*—accessible from our genealogy page.

Are they buried in Greenhill Cemetery in Laramie? If so, what location?

_____

OK, how about the online *Wyoming Newspaper Project?* What is the year of the last paper online?_____. If your person lived after that time, look up the prominent Laramie banker Edward Ivinson, instead.

Now—the *census.* Is your person listed in the census in the *AncestryLibrary database?* Use the family tree chart on the back of this page to list his/her parents and other family members as listed in the census. If you can't find your person, find someone else in Albany County and use the chart to list his/her immediate family, as listed on the census record you found.

OK—that's more than enough to intrigue and get any patron started.

Look at all the *links on our genealogy page* so you can refer patrons to them.

PUBLIC DOMAIN AND CREATIVE COMMONS
A GUIDE TO WORKS YOU CAN USE FREELY

DATE OF WORK	PROTECTED FROM	TERM
Created 1-1-78 or after	When work is fixed in tangible medium of expression	Life + 70 years[1] (or if work of corporate authorship, the shorter of 95 years from publication, or 120 years from creation)[2]
Published before 1923	In public domain	None
Published from 1923–63	When published with notice[3]	28 years + could be renewed for 47 years, now extended by 20 years for a total renewal of 67 years. If not so renewed, now in public domain
Published from 1964–77	When published with notice	28 years for first term; now automatic extension of 67 years for second term
Created before 1-1-78 but not published	1-1-78, the effective date of the 1976 Act which eliminated common law copyright	Life + 70 years or 12-31-2002, whichever is greater
Created before 1-1-78 but published between then and 12-31-2002	1-1-78, the effective date of the 1976 Act which eliminated common law copyright	Life + 70 years or 12-31-2047, whichever is greater

SOURCE: The University of Montana-Missoula Maureen and Mike Mansfield Library

1. Term of joint works is measured by life of the longest-lived author.

2. Works for hire and anonymous and pseudonymous works also have this term. 17 U.S.C. § 302(c).

3. Under the 1909 Act, works published without notice went into the public domain upon publication. Works published without notice between 1-1-78 and 3-1-89, effective date of the Berne Convention Implementation Act, retained copyright only if efforts to correct the accidental omission of notice was made within five years, such as by placing notice on unsold copies. 17 U.S.C. § 405. (Notes courtesy of Professor Tom Field, Franklin Pierce Law Center, and Lolly Gasaway)

BIBLIOGRAPHY

Introduction

Kyvig, David, and Myron A. Marty. *Nearby History: Exploring the Past Around You.* Nashville, TN: American Association for State and Local History, 1982.

Marquis, Kathy, and Leslie C. Waggener. "Historical Collections: Is Adding One Right for Your Public Library?" *Public Libraries* 50, no. 2 (March 2011): 42–48.

Chapter 1

Marquis, Kathy, and Leslie Waggener. "Local History Collections in Public Libraries." Survey distributed by the American Library Association. April 25, 2014.

Chapter 2

Bastian, Jeannette, Megan-Sniffin-Marinoff, and Donna Webber. *Archives in Libraries: What Librarians and Archivists Need to Know to Work Together.* Chicago: Society of American Archivists, forthcoming.

Cloonan, Michèle Valerie, ed. *Preserving Our Heritage: Perspectives from Antiquity to the Digital Age.* Chicago: ALA Neal-Schuman, 2015.

O'Toole, James M., and Richard J. Cox. *Understanding Archives and Manuscripts,* Archival Fundamental Series II. Chicago: Society of American Archivists, 2006.

RUSA's History Section represents the subject interests of reference librarians, archivists, bibliographers, genealogists, historians, and others engaged in historical reference or research. It brings together representatives of history collections in all formats from all types of libraries, archives, and historical societies. www.ala.org/rusa/sections/history.

- RUSA's Local History Committee offers an opportunity to discuss issues and concerns related to the management of local history services and collections. Activities include writing guidelines that address services, collections, and preservation of local history materials. www.ala.org/rusa/sections/history/committees/localhistory

- RUSA's Genealogy Committee provides a forum for serving the interests of genealogists and of librarians whose work is in, or related to, the field of genealogy. www.ala.org/rusa/sections/history/committees/genealogy

Chapter 3

Harden, Johanna. "Saving the Past for the Future (Part 1): Deciding What to Save for a Local History Collection." *Colorado Libraries* 27, no. 4 (Winter 2001): 43–44.

Hibner, Holly, and Mary Kelly. *Weed 'Em and Weep: Hoarding Is Not Collection Development.* PLA On-Demand Webinar, 2014.

Johnson, Peggy. *Fundamentals of Collection Development.* 3rd rev. ed. Chicago: American Library Association, 2014.

Nelson, Sandra, and June Garcia. *Creating Policies for Results: From Chaos to Clarity.* Chicago: American Library Association, 2003.

Pierce, Jennifer Burek. "History Is Its Own Reward Back Home in Indiana." *American Libraries* 34, no. 7 (2003): 46–48.

Sauer, Cynthia K. "Doing the Best We Can? The Use of Collection Development Policies and Cooperative Collecting Activities at Manuscript Repositories." *American Archivist* 64, no. 2 (Fall/Winter 2001): 308–49.

Shires, Nancy Patterson. "The Case for Digitizing Fiction with History." *North Carolina Libraries* 60, no. 3 (2002): 46–52.

Wallace, Linda K. *Libraries, Mission & Marketing: Writing Mission Statements That Work.* Chicago: American Library Association, 2004.

Zampaglione, Tracy, and Renae Bennett. "Electronically Preserving Obituaries." *Public Libraries* 51, no. 2 (2012): 28–30.

RUSA Guidelines for Developing Beginning Genealogical Collections and Services. The guidelines address collection development, personnel, access, and fiscal considerations for genealogical services. www.ala.org/rusa/resources/guidelines/guidelinesdeveloping.

A sample of library mission statements is provided by the Mid-Hudson (New York) Library System at http://midhudson.org/department/member_information/missions.htm.

Below are URLs of collection development policies from libraries in the United States. Although these policies may provide guidelines for collecting materials outside the scope of this book, the construction of the policies may be of assistance to you:

- Burlington (Massachusetts) Local History Collection Development Policy (www.burlington.org/departments/library/about/docs/LocalHistoryCollectionDevelopmentPolicy06.pdf)

- Monterey (California) Public Library, Collection Development Policy (www.monterey.org/Portals/2/PDFs/Policies/Policy%20401%20Collection%20Development.pdf)—pages 20–23 pertain to the library's local history collection

- Palos Verdes (California) Public Library, Local History Policies (www.pvld.org/localhistory/policies)

- Parchment (Michigan) Community Library Local History Collection, Collection Development Policy (www.parchmentlibrary.org/parchment/documents/local%20history%20collection%20development%20policy.pdf)

- Norfolk (Virginia) Public Library Sargeant Memorial Room for Local History and Genealogy, Collection Development Policy (www.norfolkpubliclibrary.org/home/showdocument?id = 20)

- Somerville (Massachusetts) Public Library, Local History Collection Development Policy (www.somervillepubliclibrary.org/localhistory/policy.html)

- Stoughton (Wisconsin) Public Library Collecting Policies, including the Kvamme Local History Collection (www.stoughtonpubliclibrary.org/POLICIES/Collection%20Development%20Approved%20%2007–18–12.pdf)

Chapter 4

Brown, Charles, Belinda Yff, and Candace Rogers. "The Library Survey: Friend or Foe? Lessons Learned Designing and Implementing User Surveys." *Kentucky Libraries* 75, no. 1 (Winter 2011): 22–25. http://sc.akronlibrary.org/wp-content/blogs.dir/19/files/2011/07/User-surveys-friend-or-foe.pdf.

Cairn, Rich. "Primary Sources: At the Heart of the Common Core State Standards." *The Teaching with Primary Sources Journal,* 2012. www.loc.gov/teachers/tps/journal/common_core/article.html.

Champagne, Matthew. *The Survey Playbook: How to Create the Perfect Survey.* Vol. 1. [United States]: CreateSpace Independent Publishing Platform, 2014.

Fink, Arlene, and Jacqueline B. Kosecoff. *How to Conduct Surveys: A Step-by-Step Guide.* 5th ed. Los Angeles: SAGE, 2013.

Fletcher, Donna, and Paula M. Singer. *The Elusive Library Non-User: How Can Libraries Find Out What Non-Users Want?* PLA On-Demand Webinar, 2012.

Chapter 5

Baranowski, Richard. "American Legion Posts: A Source of Local History for Public Libraries." *Public Libraries* 45, no. 4 (2006): 42–46.

Grover, Robert, and American Association of School Librarians. *Collaboration.* AASL Lessons Learned Series. Chicago: American Association of School Librarians, 1996.

Horton, Valerie, and Greg Pronevitz, eds. *Library Consortia: Models for Collaboration and Sustainability.* Chicago: American Library Association, 2015.

Lenstra, Noah. "Digital Roots: Community Approaches to Local and Family History." *ILA Reporter* 30, no. 3 (2012): 10–13. www.ila.org/Reporter/June2012/Reporter_0612.pdf.

Maine Memory Network (n.d.). Our Partners: Contributing Organizations and Communities. www.mainememory.net/our_partners/.

Maxwell, Nancy Kalikow. *Grant Money through Collaborative Partnerships.* Chicago: American Library Association, 2012.

Nickerson, Matthew F. "Online Multimedia Museum Exhibits: A Case Study in Technology and Collaboration." *Library Hi Tech* 22, no. 3 (2004): 270–76.

Porteus, Katie. "Bringing History to Life: School and Public Library Collaboration." *Ohio Media Spectrum* 66, no. 1 (2014): 20–22.

Smallwood, Carol. *Librarians as Community Partners: An Outreach Handbook.* Chicago: American Library Association, 2010.

Staley, Elizabeth. "Programming to Promote Local History: Remembering the Topeka Tornado of 1966." *Public Libraries* 43, no. 3 (May/June 2004): 161–64.

Chapter 6

Bryan, Cheryl. *Managing Facilities for Results: Optimizing Space for Services.* Chicago: American Library Association, 2007.

Driggers, Preston, and Eileen Dumas. *Managing Library Volunteers.* 2nd ed. Chicago: American Library Association, 2011.

Gillespie, Kellie M. *Teen Volunteer Services in Libraries.* Lanham, MD: Voya Books, 2004.

Green, Sonya L., and Thomas H. Teper. "The Importance of Disaster Planning for the Small Public Library." *Public Library Quarterly* 25, no. 3/4 (2006): 47–59.

Greenfield, Jane. *The Care of Fine Books.* New York: Skyhorse, 2007.

Halsted, Deborah D., Shari C. Clifton, and Daniel T. Wilson. *Library as Safe Haven: Disaster Planning, Response, and Recovery: A How-to-Do-It Manual for Librarians.* New York: ALA Neal-Schuman, 2014.

Kahn, Miriam B. *Disaster Response and Planning for Libraries.* 3rd ed. Chicago: American Library Association, 2012.

Landau, Herbert B. *Winning Library Grants: A Game Plan.* Chicago: American Library Association, 2010.

MacKellar, Pamela H., and Stephanie K. Gerding. *Winning Grants: A How-to-Do-It Manual for Librarians with Multimedia Tutorials and Grant Development Tools.* New York: ALA Neal-Schuman, 2010.

McCune, Bonnie F., and Charleszine Nelson. *Recruiting and Managing Volunteers in Libraries: A How-to-Do-It Manual for Librarians.* New York: ALA Neal-Schuman, 1995.

Maxwell, Nancy Kalikow. *The ALA Book of Library Grant Money.* 9th ed. Chicago: American Library Association, 2014.

Pearson, Peter. *Friends & Foundations: What They Do and How to Make the Most of Them.* PLA On-Demand Webinar, 2014.

Pearson, Peter, and Sue Hall. *Fundraising 101.* PLA On-Demand Webinar, 2014.

Rettig, Patricia J. "Water Tables: A Case Study of a Successful Fund-Raising Event." *American Archivist* 73, no. 1 (2010): 204–18.

Staines, Gail M. *Go Get That Grant!: A Practical Guide for Libraries and Nonprofit Organizations.* Lanham, MD: Scarecrow, 2010.

Summerfield Hammerman, Susan. *Researching Prospective Donors: Get More Funding for Your Library.* Chicago: American Library Association, 2014.

Swan, James. *Fundraising for Libraries: 25 Proven Ways to Get More Money for Your Library.* New York: ALA Neal-Schuman, 2002.

Wilkinson, Frances C., Linda K. Lewis, and Nancy K. Dennis. *Comprehensive Guide to Emergency and Disaster Preparedness and Recovery.* Chicago: Association of College and Research Libraries, 2010.

Chapter 7

Hendrickson, Nancy. *Unofficial Guide to Ancestry.com: How to Find Your Family History on the No. 1 Genealogy Website.* Cincinnati, OH: Family Tree Books, 2014.

Mannix, Mary K., and Fred Burchsted. *Guide to Reference in Genealogy and Biography.* Chicago: American Library Association, 2015.

Richey, Nancy. "Select Genealogy Sites for Librarians: A Survey." *Reference Reviews* 27, no. 7 (2013): 5–9.

Shires, Nancy Patterson. "To the Benefit of Both: Academic Librarians Connect with Middle School Teachers through a Digitized History Resources Workshop." *Information Technology and Libraries* 24, no. 3 (2004): 142–47.

Simpson, Jack. *Basics of Genealogy Reference: A Librarian's Guide.* Westport, CT: Libraries Unlimited, 2008.

Sowers, William R. "Bigger Things from Smaller Packages: Enhancing a Catalog with Local and Family History Analytics." *Technicalities* 23, no. 6 (2003): 1, 11–14.

Tetterton, Beverly. "Unusual Requests for Local History Collections." *North Carolina Libraries* (online), vol. 58, no. 1 (Spring/Summer 2000): 7–9.

Chapter 8

Barber, Peggy, and Linda Wallace. *Building a Buzz: Libraries and Word-of-Mouth Marketing.* Chicago: American Library Association, 2010.

Blake, Barbara, Robert S. Martin, and Yunfei Du. *Successful Community Outreach: A How-to-Do-It Manual for Librarians.* New York: ALA Neal-Schuman, 2011.

Cigler, Christine Niels. *Marketing Plans for the Faint of Heart.* PLA On-Demand Webinar, 2014.

Crawford, Walt. *Successful Social Networking in Public Libraries.* Chicago: American Library Association, 2014.

Dowd, Nancy, Mary Evangeliste, and Jonathan Silberman. *Bite-Sized Marketing: Realistic Solutions for the Overworked Librarian.* Chicago: American Library Association, 2010.

Gould, Mark, ed. *The Library PR Handbook: High Impact Communications.* Chicago: American Library Association, 2009.

Heyliger, Sean, Juli McLoone, and Nikki Lynn Thomas. "Making Connections: A Survey of Special Collections' Social Media Outreach." *American Archivist* 76, no. 2 (2013): 374–414.

James, Russell D., and Peter J. Wosh. *Public Relations and Marketing for Archives.* Chicago and New York: Society of American Archivists and Neal-Schuman, 2011.

MacRitchie, John. "The Manly Art of Local Studies Blogging: A New Approach to Old Stories." *APLIS* 25, no. 2 (2012): 89–93.

Potter, Ned. *The Library Marketing Toolkit.* London: Facet, 2012. Also look at www .librarymarketingtoolkit.com/.

Robinson, Leith. "Improving the Image of Local Studies Collections in Public Libraries." *The Australian Library Journal* 55, no. 1 (2006): 48–53.

Schull, Diantha Dow. *Archives Alive: Expanding Engagement with Public Library Archives and Special Collections.* Chicago: American Library Association, 2015.

Solomon, Laura. *The Librarian's Nitty-Gritty Guide to Social Media.* Chicago: American Library Association, 2013.

Yacovelli, Steve. *Face-to-Face Presentation Skills: How to Present Like a Lion (Even If You Feel Like a Lamb).* PLA On-Demand Webinar, 2013.

There is a Facebook group for library marketing folks hosted by Nancy Dowd and the crew at LibraryAware. If you'd like to join the group and share library marketing ideas and info, visit the page and click the join/request membership link.

Chapter 9

Association for Library Collections and Technical Services, Preservation and Reformatting Section. "Minimum Digitization Capture Recommendations." *The Association for Library Collections and Technical Services.* 2013. www.ala .org/alcts/resources/preserv/minimum-digitization-capture-recommendations.

Bernd-Klodt, Menzi, and Christopher Prom, eds. *Rights in the Digital Era.* Chicago: Society of American Archivists, 2015.

Conrad, Suzanna K. "Documenting Local History: A Case Study in Digital Storytelling." *Library Review* 62, no. 8/9 (2013): 459–71.

Crews, Kenneth D. *Copyright Law for Librarians and Educators: Creative Strategies and Practical Solutions.* 3rd ed. Chicago: American Library Association, 2012.

Dryden, Jean. "The Role of Copyright in Selection for Digitization." *American Archivist* 77, no. 1 (2014): 64–95.

Hirtle, Peter B., Emily Hudson, and Andrew T. Kenyon. *Copyright and Cultural Institutions: Guidelines for Digitization for U.S. Libraries, Archives, and Museums.* Ithaca, NY: Cornell University Library, 2009.

Kriesberg, Adam. "Increasing Access in 140 Characters or Less; or, What Are Archival Institutions Doing on Twitter?" *American Archivist* 77, no. 2 (2014): 534–57.

Lacher-Feldman, Jessica L. *Exhibits in Archives and Special Collections Libraries.* Chicago: Society of American Archivists, 2013.

Lalonde, Katy, Chris Sanagan, and Sean Smith. "The War of 1812 in 140 Characters or Less: 'Supercool or Super Un-Tweet Worthy?'" *American Archivist* 77, no. 2 (2014): 558–68.

Litzer, Don, and Andy Barnett. "Local History in E-Books and on the Web: One Library's Experience as Example and Model." *Reference & User Services Quarterly* 43, no. 3 (2004): 248–57.

Ng, Kwong Bor. *Digitization in the Real World: Lessons Learned from Small and Medium-Sized Digitization Projects.* New York: Metropolitan New York Library Council, 2010.

Sims, Nancy. *Copyright: What You REALLY Need to Know.* PLA On-Demand Webinar, 2012.

Theimer, Kate. *Web 2.0 Tools and Strategies for Archives and Local History Collections.* New York: Neal-Schuman, 2010.

Westbrook, Nicci, "Digital Collections." In *Technology for Small and One-Person Libraries: A LITA Guide,* by Rene J. Erlandson and Rachel A. Erb. New York: American Library Association, 2013.

INDEX